My Granny's Baking Book

My Granny's Baking Book

80 TRADITIONAL FAMILY RECIPES
SHOWN IN 220 PHOTOGRAPHS

CATHERINE BEST

southwater

This edition is published by Southwater,
an imprint of Anness Publishing Ltd,
Blaby Road, Wigston,
Leicestershire LE18 4SE;
info@anness.com

www.southwaterbooks.com; www.annesspublishing.com

If you like the images in this book and would like to investigate using them
for publishing, promotions or advertising, please visit our website
www.practicalpictures.com for more information.

Publisher: Joanna Lorenz
Executive Editor: Joanne Rippin
Designer: Adelle Morris
Recipes supplied by Catherine Atkinson, Janez Bogataj, Judith Dern,
Matthew Drennan, Brian Glover, Silvena Johan Lauta, Janet Lawrence,
Elena Makhonko, Maggie Mayhew, Ewa Michalik, Janny de Moor,
Anna Mosseson, Carol Pastor, Andy Parle, Mirko Trenkner, Jennie Shapter,
Christopher Trotter, Biddy White Lennon, Annette Yates and
Suzanne Vandyke.
Photography by Martin Brigdale, William Lingwood, Charlie Richards,
Craig Robertson, Debi Treloar and Jon Whitaker.

© Anness Publishing Ltd 2013

NOTES
Bracketed terms are intended for American readers.
For all recipes, quantities are given in both metric and imperial measures
and, where appropriate, in standard cups and spoons. Follow one set of
measures, but not a mixture, because they are not interchangeable.
Standard spoon and cup measures are level. 1 tsp = 5ml, 1 tbsp = 15ml,
1 cup = 250ml/8fl oz.
Australian standard tablespoons are 20ml. Australian readers should use
3 tsp in place of 1 tbsp for measuring small quantities.
American pints are 16fl oz/2 cups. American readers should use 20fl oz/
2.5 cups in place of 1 pint when measuring liquids.
Electric oven temperatures in this book are for conventional ovens. When
using a fan oven, the temperature will probably need to be reduced by
about 10–20°C/20–40°F. Since ovens vary, you should check with your
manufacturer's instruction book for guidance.
The nutritional analysis given for each recipe is calculated per portion
(i.e. serving or item), unless otherwise stated. If the recipe gives a range,
such as Serves 4–6, then the nutritional analysis will be for the smaller
portion size, i.e. 6 servings. The analysis does not include optional
ingredients, such as salt added to taste.
Medium (US large) eggs are used unless otherwise stated.

PUBLISHER'S NOTE
Although the advice and information in this book are believed to be accurate
and true at the time of going to press, neither the authors nor the publisher
can accept any legal responsibility or liability for any errors or omissions that
may have been made nor for any inaccuracies nor for any loss, harm or
injury that comes about from following instructions or advice in this book.

CONTENTS

INTRODUCTION

The idea of baking with Granny conjures up a vision of a warm, friendly home suffused with the aroma of bread and cakes, where there's always a cosy welcome and plenty of goodies to eat. But this pleasant snapshot of the kitchens of the past does not tell the whole story. The cooking of previous generations also has plenty to teach us in terms of eating seasonal, local food and preserving ingredients wisely, rediscovering the joy of culinary traditions that have been passed down through the decades.

The basic cookery techniques and the unbroken heritage of recipes that our grandmothers learned from their mothers are as important today as they ever were, and we should play our part in passing them on to the next generation. From using seasonal food and local ingredients, to baking celebration cakes and cherishing kitchen equipment that lasted a lifetime – our ancestors knew how important these things were for the well-being of the whole family.

PATTERNS OF EATING

Eating patterns are usually defined by work and school; in the past people were able to come home for lunch, but now this is impractical, and most of us are out until the evening. Breakfast, and often lunch, tend to be rushed meals. Often people miss breakfast and eat a storebought sandwich at an office desk or on a bench in the park. This is part of modern life, but it also means that

Below: Afternoon tea is a time-honoured tradition that is well worth reviving.

Right: Many families have recipe collections that have been handed down.

the evening meal is our most important one of the day, where we will make an effort to sit down with family or friends. Weekends offer valuable time to spend in the kitchen, when we can bake a cake and invite people round for tea, create a lovely treat for the children, or stock up for the week ahead.

To fill the hunger gap between meals, there are plenty of recipes in this book for healthy snacks, like fruit-filled cakes, sweet breads and cookies that would once have been served for afternoon tea. Teatime may not be quite the institution it was, but the recipes remain and are universally popular, particularly with children.

FAMILY TRADITIONS

In many families, a folder or box of handwritten recipes exists, handed down from one generation to the next. Splashed with gravy, worn at the corners and annotated by the cook, these recipes represent each family's

collective memory. Celebration bakes are the most evocative element of a family's traditions. At Christmas, Easter or Thanksgiving, and for birthdays, weddings or christenings, families create their own favourite dishes and rituals that are called for each year.

ABOUT THIS BOOK

The welcoming warmth and bounty of a grandmother's kitchen is re-created here in this collection of recipes. Grandmothers are especially renowned for their baking, and the chapters here on mouthwatering desserts, cakes, biscuits and cookies give recipes from the lightest sponge cake to a rib-sticking tea loaf. With such a wealth of well-loved traditional recipes, you will be able to make the kitchen the heart of your own home.

Right: Stocking baking ingredients in the storecupboard or pantry means you will always have what you need for delicious cakes, cookies and bakes.

DESSERTS

Nothing quite beats a proper pudding at the end of a meal, and it brings a smile to everyone's face, from the youngest to the oldest. This chapter holds a whole treasure trove of favourite desserts and puddings from past times to be explored — hot pies, crumbles, sponges and suet puddings, as well as chilled fruit fools and sorbets — something for every occasion and every season.

DEEP-DISH APPLE PIE

PERHAPS THE DESSERT WE MOST ASSOCIATE WITH HOME, NO-ONE CAN RESIST A REALLY GOOD APPLE PIE, TOPPED WITH CRUMBLY HOME-MADE SHORTCRUST PASTRY. IN THIS RECIPE THE APPLES ARE TOSSED IN CARAMEL BUTTER BEFORE BAKING TO MAKE THEM EVEN MORE IRRESISTIBLE.

2 Peel, core and thickly slice the apples. Melt the butter in a frying pan, add the sugar and cook for 3–4 minutes, until melted and caramelized.

3 Add the apples to the pan and stir around to coat. Cook over a brisk heat until the apples take on a little colour, add the spice mixture and tip out into a bowl to cool slightly.

4 Divide the pastry in two and, on a lightly floured surface, roll into two rounds to fit a deep 23cm/9in pie plate. Line the plate with one round of pastry. Spoon in the apples and mound up in the centre.

SERVES 6

INGREDIENTS
  900g/2lb eating apples
  75g/3oz/6 tbsp unsalted butter
  45–60ml/3–4 tbsp demerara
    (raw) sugar
  2.5ml/½ tsp mixed (apple pie)
    spice
For the pastry
  250g/9oz/2¼ cups plain
    (all-purpose) flour
  pinch of salt
  50g/2oz/¼ cup white cooking fat,
    chilled and diced
  75g/3oz/6 tbsp unsalted butter,
    chilled and diced
  30–45ml/2–3 tbsp chilled water
  a little milk, for brushing
  caster (superfine) sugar,
    for dredging

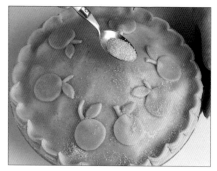

1 Preheat the oven to 200°C/400°F/ Gas 6. Make the pastry first. Sift the flour and salt into a bowl. Rub in the fat and butter until the mixture resembles fine breadcrumbs. Stir in enough chilled water to bring the pastry together. Knead lightly then wrap in cling film (plastic wrap) and chill for 30 minutes.

5 Cover with the remaining pastry, sealing and crimping the edges. Make a slit on the top of the pastry to allow steam to escape. Brush the pie with milk and dredge with caster sugar.

6 Bake in the oven for 25–35 minutes until golden and firm. Serve with clotted cream or ice cream.

Energy 591Kcal/2488kJ; Protein 7.4g; Carbohydrate 89.9g, of which sugars 39.8g; Fat 25g, of which saturates 15.3g; Cholesterol 62mg; Calcium 117mg; Fibre 4.4g; Sodium 193mg.

BAKEWELL TART

THIS TRADITIONAL TART COMES ORIGINALLY FROM THE DERBYSHIRE VILLAGE OF BAKEWELL, WHERE IT IS KNOWN AS BAKEWELL PUDDING. A CRISP PASTRY SHELL IS TOPPED WITH JAM AND THEN A LIGHT ALMOND SPONGE. IT CAN BE SERVED AT TEA TIME OR AS A SPECIAL DESSERT WITH CREAM.

SERVES 4

INGREDIENTS
    225g/8oz puff pastry
    30ml/2 tbsp raspberry or apricot
      jam
    2 eggs, plus 2 egg yolks
    115g/4oz/½ cup caster (superfine)
      sugar
    115g/4oz/½ cup butter, melted
    50g/2oz/⅔ cup ground almonds
    a few drops of almond extract
    icing (confectioners') sugar,
      for dusting

1 Preheat the oven to 200°C/400°F Gas 6. Roll out the pastry on a lightly floured surface and use to line an 18cm/7in pie plate. Trim the edge.

2 Prick the pastry case all over, then spread the jam over the base. Collect up the pastry trimmings.

3 Re-roll the trimmings and cut out wide strips of pastry. Use these to decorate the edge of the pastry case by gently twisting them around the rim, joining the strips together as necessary. Brushing the edge with a little milk first will help the pastry hold.

GRANDMOTHER'S TIP
Since this pastry case is not baked blind before being filled, place a baking sheet in the oven while it preheats, then place the tart on the hot sheet. This will ensure that the base of the pastry case cooks right through.

4 Whisk the eggs, egg yolks and sugar together in a bowl until the mixture is thick and pale. Gently stir the melted butter, ground almonds and almond essence into the whisked egg mixture.

5 Pour the mixture into the pastry case and bake for 30 minutes, or until the filling is just set and is lightly browned. Dust with icing sugar before serving hot, warm or cold.

Energy 700Kcal/2919kJ; Protein 10.8g; Carbohydrate 57.1g, of which sugars 36.7g; Fat 49.9g, of which saturates 17.1g; Cholesterol 257g; Calcium 110mg; Fibre 0.9g; Sodium 394mg.

FRESH PLUM TART

THIS SPECIAL DESSERT WOULD WORK SPLENDIDLY AS THE FINAL FLOURISH AFTER A FAMILY SUNDAY DINNER. THE CIRCLES OF SLICED PLUMS ARE SET IN A TASTY SWEET YEAST DOUGH, WHICH IS A LITTLE MORE COMPLICATED TO MAKE THAN A PASTRY CASE, BUT IS WELL WORTH THE EXTRA EFFORT.

SERVES 6–8

INGREDIENTS
    250g/9oz/2¼ cups plain (all-purpose)
      flour, plus extra for dusting
    50g/2oz/¼ cup caster (superfine)
      sugar
    15ml/1 tbsp easy-blend (rapid-rise)
      dried yeast
    2.5ml/½ tsp salt
    1 egg, beaten
    100ml/3½fl oz/scant ½ cup milk
    50–75g/2–3oz/4–6 tbsp unsalted
      butter, softened
For the filling
    675g/1½lb fresh ripe plums, quartered
    60ml/4 tbsp soft light brown sugar
    15ml/1 tbsp ground cinnamon
    15ml/1 tbsp rum or dessert wine
    5ml/1 tsp cornflour (cornstarch)

1 Sift the flour into a large mixing bowl. Stir in the sugar, dried yeast and salt. Make a well in the centre and pour in the beaten egg and half the milk.

2 Stir, gradually incorporating the dry ingredients until the mixture starts to hold together. Add the extra milk, if needed. Finally add the softened butter and mix with your fingertips to a soft dough.

3 On a lightly floured surface, knead the dough lightly, form it into a ball and place in a large, lightly oiled bowl. Cover with clear film (plastic wrap) and leave to rise in a warm, draught-free place for about 30 minutes or until doubled in bulk.

4 Preheat the oven to 220°C/425°F/ Gas 7. Grease a 23cm/9in loose-bottomed tart or flan tin (pan) and dust it lightly with flour.

5 Meanwhile, prepare the filling. Put the plums in a bowl. Sprinkle with 45ml/3 tbsp of the brown sugar and two-thirds of the cinnamon. Add the rum or dessert wine, and leave to stand while the dough is rising.

6 Knock back (punch down) the dough. Roll it out on a lightly floured surface and line the tart or flan tin (pan) without stretching the dough. Trim and crimp the edges and prick the base of the pastry case (pie shell) with a fork. Sprinkle the base with the remaining brown sugar and cinnamon, then leave to stand for 15 minutes.

7 Sift the cornflour over the plums, then layer them in the pastry case. Place the tin on a hot baking sheet in the oven. Bake for 30–45 minutes or until the pie is cooked and the pastry is golden brown.

8 Leave to cool on a wire rack for about 15 minutes before removing from the tin. Serve immediately, in slices.

VARIATION
Instead of plums, try other fruits for this tart, such as apricots, cherries, berries, apples or pears.

SWEET APPLE CAKE WITH HOMEMADE CUSTARD

SWEET EATING APPLES ARE BEST FOR MAKING THIS SPECIAL CAKE. THE SPICED APPLE LAYER IS BAKED UNDER A VERY LIGHT ALMOND SPONGE AND IT IS SERVED WITH A DELECTABLE FRESH CUSTARD. THIS IS AN OLD-FASHIONED RECIPE DESIGNED TO MAKE BEST USE OF AN APPLE GLUT IN THE AUTUMN.

SERVES 6-8

INGREDIENTS
    115g/4½oz/½ cup plus 1 tbsp
      unsalted (sweet) butter
    7 eating apples
    200g/7oz/1 cup caster (superfine)
      sugar, plus 30ml/2 tbsp extra
    10ml/2 tsp ground cinnamon
    2 egg yolks and 3 egg whites
    100g/4oz/1 cup ground almonds
    grated rind and juice of ½ lemon
For the vanilla cream
    250ml/8fl oz/1 cup milk
    250ml/8fl oz/1 cup double (heavy)
      cream
    15ml/1 tbsp sugar
    1 vanilla pod (bean), split
    4 egg yolks, beaten

1 Preheat the oven to 180ºC/350ºF/Gas 4. Butter a 20cm/8in flan tin (pan) using 15g/½oz/1 tbsp of the butter. Peel, core and thinly slice the apples and put the slices in a bowl.

2 Add 30ml/2 tbsp caster sugar and cinnamon to the apples, mix together, then transfer the spiced apples to the prepared tin and spread evenly.

3 Put the remaining butter and sugar in a bowl and whisk them together until they are light and fluffy.

4 Beat the egg yolks, one at a time, into the sugar and butter mixture, then stir in the ground almonds and lemon rind and juice.

5 Whisk the egg whites until stiff then fold into the mixture. Pour the mixture over the apples in the flan tin. Bake in the oven for about 40 minutes until golden brown.

6 Meanwhile, make the custard. Put the milk, cream, sugar and vanilla pod in a pan and heat gently. Add a little of the warm milk mixture to the eggs then slowly add the egg mixture to the pan and continue to heat gently, stirring all the time, until the mixture thickens. Do not allow the mixture to boil or it will curdle.

7 Remove the vanilla pod and serve the custard with the apple cake.

Energy 541kcal/2254kJ; Protein 7.6g; Carbohydrate 39.7g, of which sugars 39.3g; Fat 40.3g, of which saturates 20g; Cholesterol 227mg; Calcium 122mg; Fibre 2.1g; Sodium 135mg.

LEMON MERINGUE PIE

THIS IS SURELY ONE OF THE MOST POPULAR ITEMS ON THE DESSERT MENU. THE FRESH LEMONY FLAVOUR WAS ESPECIALLY RELISHED AFTER WARTIME RATIONING, WHEN AT LAST LEMONS, SUGAR AND EGGS BECAME PLENTIFUL ONCE MORE AND THIS DELIGHTFUL PIE WAS REDISCOVERED.

5 Remove the parchment or foil, return the pastry to the oven and cook for a further 5 minutes. Reduce the temperature to 150°C/300°F/Gas 2.

6 To make the lemon filling, put the cornflour into a pan and add the sugar, lemon rind and 300ml/½ pint/1¼ cups water. Heat the mixture, stirring, until it comes to the boil and thickens. Reduce the heat and simmer very gently for 1 minute. Remove the pan from the heat and stir in the lemon juice.

7 Add the the egg yolks to the lemon mixture, one at a time and beating after each addition, and then stir in the butter. Pour the mixture into the pastry case (pie shell) and level the surface.

8 To make the meringue topping, whisk the egg whites until stiff peaks form, then whisk in half the sugar. Fold in the rest of the sugar using a metal spoon. Spread the meringue over the lemon filling, covering it completely. Cook for about 20 minutes until lightly browned.

SERVES 6

INGREDIENTS
For the pastry
    115g/4oz/1 cup plain (all-purpose)
        flour
    pinch of salt
    25g/1oz/2 tbsp lard, diced
    25g/1oz/2 tbsp butter, diced
For the filling
    50g/2oz/¼ cup cornflour (cornstarch)
    175g/6oz/¾ cup caster (superfine)
        sugar
    finely grated rind and juice of
        2 lemons
    2 egg yolks
    15g/½oz/1 tbsp butter, diced
For the meringue topping
    2 egg whites
    75g/3oz/½ cup caster
        (superfine) sugar

1 To make the pastry, sift the flour and salt into a bowl and add the lard and butter. With the fingertips, lightly rub the fats into the flour until the mixture resembles fine crumbs.

2 Stir in about 20ml/2 tbsp cold water until the mixture can be gathered together into a smooth ball of dough. (Alternatively, make the pastry using a food processor.)

3 Wrap the pastry and refrigerate for at least 30 minutes. Meanwhile, preheat the oven to 200°C/400°F/Gas 6.

4 Roll out the pastry on a lightly floured surface and use to line a 20cm/8in flan tin (pan). Prick the base with a fork, line with baking parchment or foil and bake in the oven for 15 minutes.

Energy 357Kcal/1497kJ; Protein 6.8g; Carbohydrate 42.8g, of which sugars 25.1g; Fat 18.9g, of which saturates 9g; Cholesterol 129mg; Calcium 108mg; Fibre 0.7g; Sodium 137mg.

TREACLE TART

*TRADITIONAL HOME-MADE SHORTCRUST PASTRY IS PERFECT FOR THIS OLD-FASHIONED FAVOURITE.
THE STICKY LEMON-FLAVOURED SYRUP FILLING IS TOPPED WITH TWISTED LATTICES OF LEFTOVER
PASTRY FOR A REALLY AUTHENTIC LOOK. IT CAN BE SERVED WARM OR COLD WITH CUSTARD OR CREAM.*

SERVES 4-6

INGREDIENTS
260g/9½oz/generous ¾ cup golden
(light corn) syrup
75g/3oz/1½ cups fresh
white breadcrumbs
grated rind of 1 lemon
30ml/2 tbsp lemon juice
For the pastry
150g/5oz/1¼ cups plain (all-purpose)
flour
2.5ml/½ tsp salt
130g/4½oz/9 tbsp chilled butter,
diced
45–60/3–4 tbsp chilled water

1 To make the pastry, combine the
flour and salt in a bowl. Rub or cut in
the butter until the mixture resembles
coarse breadcrumbs.

2 With a fork, stir in just enough water
to bind the dough. Gather into a smooth
ball, knead lightly for a few seconds
until smooth, then wrap in clear film
(plastic wrap) and chill for 20 minutes.

3 On a lightly floured surface, roll out
the pastry to a thickness of 3mm/⅛in.
Transfer to a 20cm/8in fluted flan tin
(quiche pan) and trim off the overhang.
Chill the pastry case (pie shell), for 20
minutes. Reserve the pastry trimmings.

4 Put a baking sheet in the oven and
preheat to 200°C/400°F/Gas 6. To make
the filling, begin by warming the syrup
in a pan until it melts.

5 Remove the syrup from the heat and
stir in the breadcrumbs and lemon rind.
Leave to stand for 10 minutes, then add
more breadcrumbs if the mixture is too
thin and moist. Stir in the lemon juice,
then spread the mixture evenly in the
pastry case.

6 Roll out the pastry trimmings and cut
into 10–12 thin strips.

7 Twist the strips into spirals, then lay
half of them on the filling. Arrange the
remaining strips at right angles to form
a lattice. Press the ends on to the rim.

8 Place the tart on the hot baking
sheet and bake for 10 minutes. Lower
the oven temperature to 190°C/375°F/
Gas 5. Bake for 15 minutes more, until
golden. Serve warm or cold.

Energy 420Kcal/1764kJ; Protein 4.1g; Carbohydrate 63.5g, of which sugars 35.1g; Fat 18.4g, of which saturates 11.3g; Cholesterol 46g; Calcium 62mg; Fibre 1.1g; Sodium 344mg.

ONE-CRUST RHUBARB PIE

THIS IS SUCH AN EASY PIE TO MAKE, AND IT CAN BE FILLED WITH ALL KINDS OF FRUIT. IT DOESN'T MATTER HOW ROUGH THE PIE LOOKS WHEN IT GOES INTO THE OVEN — THE UNEVENNESS OF THE PASTRY IS PART OF ITS CHARM. TOPPED WITH A SPRINKLING OF SUGAR, IT IS THE PERFECT RUSTIC PUDDING.

SERVES 6

INGREDIENTS
    350g/12oz ready-made shortcrust
        pastry, thawed if frozen
    1 egg yolk, beaten
    25g/1oz/3 tbsp semolina
    25g/1oz/¼ cup hazelnuts, coarsely
        chopped
    30ml/2 tbsp golden granulated sugar
For the filling
    450g/1lb rhubarb, cut into
        2.5cm/1in pieces
    75g/3oz/⅓ cup caster (superfine)
        sugar
    1–2 pieces stem ginger in syrup,
        drained and finely chopped

GRANDMOTHER'S TIP
Egg yolk glaze brushed on to pastry gives it a nice golden sheen. However, be careful not to drip the glaze on the baking sheet, or it will burn.

1 Preheat the oven to 200°C/400°F/ Gas 6. Roll out the pastry to a circle 35cm/14in across. Lay it over the rolling pin and transfer it to a large baking sheet. Brush a little egg yolk over the pastry. Scatter the semolina over the centre, leaving a wide rim all round.

2 Make the filling. Place the rhubarb pieces, caster sugar and chopped ginger in a large bowl and mix well.

3 Pile the rhubarb mixture into the middle of the pastry. Fold the rim roughly over the filling so that it almost covers it. Some of the fruit will remain visible in the centre.

4 Glaze the pastry rim with any remaining egg yolk and scatter the hazelnuts and golden sugar over. Bake for 30–35 minutes or until the pastry is golden brown. Serve warm.

Energy 389Kcal/1633kJ; Protein 5.6g; Carbohydrate 49.7g, of which sugars 19.6g; Fat 20.1g, of which saturates 5.6g; Cholesterol 42g; Calcium 139mg; Fibre 2.5g; Sodium 239mg.

APPLE AND BLACKBERRY CRUMBLE

AUTUMN HERALDS THE HARVEST OF APPLES AND OTHER SUCCULENT FRUITS. THE PERFECT COMPANION TO THE SWEET APPLES IS A BASKET OF TART LITTLE BLACKBERRIES FROM THE FIELD EDGES. FINELY TEXTURED OATMEAL IS ADDED TO THE CRUMBLE TOPPING FOR AN EXTRA NUTRITIOUS CRUNCH.

SERVES 6–8

INGREDIENTS
  900g/2lb cooking apples
  450g/1lb/4 cups blackberries
  squeeze of lemon juice (optional)
  175g/6oz/scant 1 cup granulated
    (white) sugar
For the topping
  115g/4oz/½ cup butter
  115g/4oz/1 cup wholemeal
    (whole-wheat) flour
  50g/2oz/½ cup fine or medium
    pinhead oatmeal
  50g/2oz/¼ cup soft light brown sugar
  a little grated lemon rind (optional)

1 Preheat the oven to 200°C/400°F/ Gas 6. To make the crumble topping, rub the butter into the flour until the mixture resembles rough breadcrumbs.

GRANDMOTHER'S TIP
This delicious topping can be used with most fruits; try plums or raspberries.

2 Add the oatmeal and brown sugar to the bowl and continue to rub in until the mixture begins to stick together, forming larger crumbs. Using a fork, mix in the grated lemon rind, if using.

3 Peel, core and slice the cooking apples into wedges.

4 Put the apples, blackberries, lemon juice (if using), 30ml/2 tbsp water and the sugar into a shallow ovenproof dish, about 2 litres/3½ pints/9 cups capacity.

5 Cover the fruit with the topping. Sprinkle with a little cold water. Bake in the oven for 15 minutes, then reduce the heat to 190°C/375°F/Gas 5 and cook for another 15–20 minutes until crunchy and brown on top. Serve hot.

Energy 470Kcal/1974kJ; Protein 5.1g; Carbohydrate 78.2g, of which sugars 60.3g; Fat 17.2g, of which saturates 10g; Cholesterol 41mg; Calcium 71mg; Fibre 7g; Sodium 128mg.

STICKY COFFEE AND GINGER PUDDING

GINGER HAS BEEN USED IN BOTH SWEET AND SAVOURY COOKING FOR CENTURIES. HERE IT IS BLENDED WITH COFFEE TO FLAVOUR THE FEATHER-LIGHT SPONGE. WHEN THE PUDDING IS TURNED OUT, THE COFFEE AND GINGER SAUCE WILL TRICKLE DOWN THE SIDES. SERVE WITH CREAM OR ICE CREAM.

2 Put the ground coffee in a small bowl. Heat the ginger syrup until almost boiling; pour into the coffee. Stir well and leave for 4 minutes. Pour through a sieve (strainer) into the heatproof bowl.

3 In a clean bowl, beat half the caster sugar and egg yolks until light and fluffy. Fold in the sifted flour and ginger, breadcrumbs and ground almonds.

4 In a third bowl, whisk the egg whites until stiff, then gradually whisk in the remaining caster sugar. Fold this into the cake mixture. Transfer the mixture into the heatproof bowl.

SERVES 4

INGREDIENTS

- 30ml/2 tbsp soft light brown sugar
- 25g/1oz/2 tbsp stem ginger, chopped
- 30ml/2 tbsp ground coffee
- 75ml/5 tbsp stem ginger syrup (from a jar of preserved stem ginger)
- 115g/4oz/generous ½ cup caster (superfine) sugar
- 3 eggs, separated
- 25g/1oz/¼ cup plain (all-purpose) flour, sifted with 5ml/1 tsp ground ginger
- 65g/2½oz/generous 1 cup fresh white breadcrumbs
- 25g/1oz/¼ cup ground almonds

1 Preheat the oven to 180°C/350°F/ Gas 4. Grease and line the base of a 750ml/1¼ pint/3 cup heatproof bowl, then sprinkle in the soft light brown sugar and chopped stem ginger.

5 Cover the basin with a piece of pleated greased greaseproof paper and secure with string. Bake for 40 minutes, or until the sponge is firm to the touch. Turn out and serve immediately.

GRANDMOTHER'S TIP
This pudding can also be baked in a 900ml/1½ pint/3¾ cup loaf tin and served thickly sliced.

Energy 382Kcal/1617kJ; Protein 9.7g; Carbohydrate 70.6g, of which sugars 53.5g; Fat 8.9g, of which saturates 1.7g; Cholesterol 171g; Calcium 93mg; Fibre 1g; Sodium 240mg.

QUEEN OF PUDDINGS

THIS DELICATE DESSERT MAKES THE MOST OF EGGS IN THRIFTY STYLE, WITH THE YOLKS STIRRED WITH BREADCRUMBS, SUGAR AND LEMON TO FORM THE BASE AND THE WHITES BEATEN UP INTO A LIGHT MERINGUE TOPPING. THE FAMOUS MRS BEETON CALLED THIS RECIPE 'QUEEN OF BREAD PUDDING'.

SERVES 4

INGREDIENTS
 80g/3oz/1½ cups fresh breadcrumbs
 60ml/4 tbsp caster (superfine) sugar,
  plus 5ml/1 tsp
 grated rind of 1 lemon
 600ml/1 pint/2½ cups milk
 4 eggs
 45ml/3 tbsp raspberry jam, warmed

1 Stir the breadcrumbs, 30ml/2 tbsp of the sugar and the lemon rind together in a bowl. Bring the milk to the boil in a pan, then stir it into the breadcrumb and sugar mixture.

2 Separate three of the eggs and beat the yolks with the remaining whole egg.

3 Stir the eggs into the breadcrumb mixture, then pour into a buttered ovenproof dish and leave to stand for 30 minutes.

4 Meanwhile, preheat the oven to 160°C/325°F/Gas 3. Cook the pudding for 50–60 minutes, until set.

5 Whisk the egg whites in a large, clean bowl until stiff, then gradually whisk in the remaining 30ml/2 tbsp caster sugar until the mixture is thick and glossy. Be careful not to overwhip.

GRANDMOTHER'S TIP
The traditional recipe stipulates that raspberry jam should be used, but you could ring the changes by replacing it with a different jam, such as strawberry or plum, you could also use lemon curd, marmalade or fruit purée.

6 Spread the jam over the set custard, then spoon on the egg whites. Sprinkle the remaining sugar over the top, then bake for a further 15 minutes, until the meringue is light golden. Serve warm.

Energy 297kcal/1259kJ; Protein 13.7g; Carbohydrate 45g, of which sugars 31g; Fat 8.5g, of which saturates 3.2g; Cholesterol 199mg; Calcium 242mg; Fibre 0.4g; Sodium 281mg.

BREAD AND BUTTER PUDDING

PLATES OF BREAD AND BUTTER WERE A STANDARD FEATURE OF AN ENGLISH TEA OR NURSERY SUPPER IN VICTORIAN AND EDWARDIAN TIMES. FRUGAL COOKS NEEDED TO COME UP WITH WAYS TO USE UP THE LEFTOVERS, AND THIS BREAD AND BUTTER PUDDING WAS THE VERY TASTY RESULT.

SERVES 4–6

INGREDIENTS

- 50g/2oz/4 tbsp soft butter
- about 6 large slices of day-old white bread
- 50g/2oz dried fruit, such as raisins, sultanas (golden raisins) or chopped dried apricots
- 40g/1½oz/3 tbsp caster (superfine) sugar
- 2 large eggs
- 600ml/1 pint/2½ cups full cream (whole) milk

1 Preheat the oven to 160°C/325°F/Gas 5. Lightly butter a 1.2 litre/2 pint/5 cup ovenproof dish.

2 Butter the slices of bread and cut them into small triangles or squares.

3 Arrange half the bread pieces, buttered side up, in the dish. Sprinkle the dried fruit and half the sugar on top.

4 Lay the remaining bread slices, again buttered side up, evenly on top of the fruit. Sprinkle the remaining sugar evenly over the bread.

5 Beat the eggs lightly together, just to break up the yolks and whites, and stir in the milk.

6 Strain the egg mixture and pour it over the bread in the dish. Push the top slices down into the liquid if necessary so that it is evenly absorbed.

7 Leave the pudding to stand for 30 minutes to allow the bread to soak up all the liquid (this is an important step so don't be tempted to skip it).

8 Put the dish into the hot oven and cook for about 45 minutes, or until the custard is set and the top is crisp and golden brown. Serve the pudding immediately.

VARIATION

To make a special occasion chocolate bread and butter pudding, complete steps 1–4, omitting the dried fruit if you wish. Break 150g/5oz dark (bittersweet) chocolate into 500ml/17fl oz/generous 2 cups milk, and heat gently (on the stove or on low power in the microwave) until the milk is warm and the chocolate has melted. Stir frequently during heating and do not allow the milk to boil. Stir the warm chocolate milk into the beaten eggs in step 5, and then continue with the remaining steps.

Energy 622kcal/2597kJ; Protein 10.5g; Carbohydrate 55.6g, of which sugars 37.8g; Fat 39g, of which saturates 23g; Cholesterol 186mg; Calcium 203mg; Fibre 1.6g; Sodium 350mg.

RICE PUDDING <u>WITH</u> RHUBARB COMPOTE

THIS DESSERT COMBINES TWO TRADITIONAL FAVOURITES: RICE PUDDING, A YEAR-ROUND SWEET TREAT FROM THE STORE CUPBOARD, AND GENTLY COOKED ORANGE-FLAVOURED RHUBARB, AT ITS BEST IN THE SUMMER WHEN THE RHUBARB IS GROWING STRONGLY IN THE KITCHEN GARDEN.

SERVES 4

INGREDIENTS
  175g/6oz/scant 1 cup short-grain
    rice
  1 litre/1¾ pints/4 cups milk
  50g/2oz/¼ cup caster (superfine)
    sugar, plus extra for sprinkling
  5g/⅛oz vanilla sugar (about) or
    ½ tsp vanilla extract
  50g/2oz/4 tbsp butter
  pinch of salt
  pinch of ground cinnamon
For the compote
  500g/1¼lb rhubarb
  75g/3oz/⅔ cup caster (superfine)
    sugar
  juice of 1 orange
  2 pieces of star anise
  cornflour (cornstarch)

1 Wash the rice thoroughly and drain. Put the milk in a pan with the sugar, vanilla sugar, butter and salt. Bring to the boil, then reduce the heat and add the rice.

2 Cook gently for about 15 minutes, stirring constantly, until the rice is cooked. Turn into a serving dish and sprinkle with sugar, mixed with ground cinnamon. Keep warm.

GRANDMOTHER'S TIP
This rice pudding is also delicious if served cold. Simply make both the rice pudding and the fruit compote in advance, and chill both in the refrigerator before serving.

3 While the rice cooks, cut the rhubarb stems into pieces 2cm/¾in thick.

4 Heat a heavy pan over a medium heat and pour in the sugar. Heat the sugar until it starts to dissolve, and slightly caramelizes, then remove from the heat, stir in the orange juice and add the star anise.

5 Return the pan to the heat, add the rhubarb, bring to the boil, then reduce the heat and simmer for 8–10 minutes.

6 If there is too much juice, add a little cornflour slaked in a spoonful of cold water and cook until the sauce has thickened. Serve the rice with the rhubarb.

Energy 557Kcal/2348kJ; Protein 12g; Carbohydrate 80g, of which sugars 45g; Fat 21g, of which saturates 12g; Cholesterol 61mg; Calcium 394mg; Fibre 2g; Sodium 244mg.

JAM ROLY POLY

THIS WARMING WINTER PUDDING, MADE WITH JAM SPREAD INSIDE A SUET PASTRY ROLL, FIRST APPEARED IN THE 19TH CENTURY. IT CAN BE MADE WITH A SWEET OR SAVOURY FILLING, BUT THIS SWEET VERSION WILL UNDOUBTEDLY BE THE CHILDREN'S FAVOURITE. SERVE IT WITH CREAMY CUSTARD.

SERVES 4–6

INGREDIENTS
175g/6oz/1½ cups self-raising
  (self-rising) flour
pinch of salt
75g/3oz shredded suet (or vegetarian
  equivalent)
finely grated rind of 1 small lemon
90ml/6 tbsp strawberry jam

1 Preheat the oven to 180°C/350°F/ Gas 4 and line a baking sheet with baking parchment.

2 Sift the flour and salt into a bowl and stir in the suet and lemon rind. Stir in just enough cold water to enable you to gather the mixture into a ball of soft dough, finishing off with your fingers.

3 Remove the ball of dough from the bowl, and on a lightly floured work surface or board, knead it very lightly until smooth.

4 Gently roll out the pastry into a rectangle that measures approximately 30 x 20cm/12 x 8in.

5 Using a palette knife or metal spatula, spread the jam evenly over the pastry, leaving the side edges and ends clear.

6 Brush the edges of the pastry with a little water and, starting at one of the short ends, carefully roll up the pastry. Try to keep the roll fairly loose so that the jam is not squeezed out.

7 Place the roll, seam side down, on the prepared baking sheet. Put into the hot oven and cook for 30–40 minutes until risen, golden brown and cooked through. Leave the pudding to cool for a few minutes before cutting into thick slices to serve.

GRANDMOTHER'S TIP
For the lightest suet pastry, use as little cold water as possible to mix the dough, and handle it as gently and lightly as you can.

VARIATION
To make a steamed pudding, try the traditional nursery favourite, Spotted Dick, replace half the flour with 115g/4oz/2 cups fresh white breadcrumbs; add 50g/2oz/¼ cup caster (superfine) sugar and 175g/6oz/¾ cup currants to the flour in step 2.

Instead of water to mix, use about 75ml/5 tbsp milk. Leave out the jam and just form into a sausage shape without rolling.

Shape the mixture into a roll and wrap loosely (to allow room for the pudding to rise and expand) first in baking parchment and then in a large sheet of foil. Twist the ends of the paper and foil to seal them securely and tie a string handle from one end to the other.

Lower the package into a wide pan of boiling water on the stove, cover and boil for about 1½ hours. Check the water level occasionally and top up with boiling water if necessary. Serve the pudding hot with custard.

Energy 240kcal/1008kJ; Protein 2.8g; Carbohydrate 33.7g, of which sugars 10.7g; Fat 11.3g, of which saturates 5.7g; Cholesterol 0mg; Calcium 104mg; Fibre 0.9g; Sodium 111mg.

LEMON SURPRISE PUDDING

THE SURPRISE IN THIS PUDDING IS THE POOL OF TANGY LEMON SAUCE THAT FORMS DURING COOKING BENEATH A LIGHT SPONGE TOPPING. A FEW SIMPLE INGREDIENTS WORK THEIR MAGIC TO MAKE A SPECIAL DESSERT THAT CHILDREN WILL LOVE, WITH A DELICIOUS TASTE AND TEXTURE.

2 Beat the butter and sugar together in a large bowl until pale and fluffy. Beat in one egg yolk at a time and gradually add in the lemon rind and juice until well mixed; do not worry if the mixture curdles a little.

3 Sift the flour and stir it into the lemon mixture until well mixed, then gradually stir in the milk.

4 Whisk the egg whites in a separate bowl until stiff, but not dry, then lightly, but thoroughly, fold into the lemon mixture in three batches. Carefully pour the mixture into the soufflé dish, then pour boiling water into the roasting pan.

5 Bake the pudding in the middle of the oven for 45 minutes, or until golden on top. Dust with icing (confectioners') sugar and serve immediately.

SERVES 4

INGREDIENTS
75g/3oz/6 tbsp butter
175g/6oz/¾ cup soft light
  brown sugar
4 eggs, separated
grated rind and juice of 4 lemons
50g/2oz/½ cup self-raising
  (self-rising) flour
120ml/4fl oz/½ cup milk

1 Preheat the oven to 180°C/350°F/ Gas 4. Butter an 18cm/7in soufflé dish and stand it in a roasting pan.

VARIATION
This pudding is also delicious made with oranges instead of lemons.

GRANDMOTHER'S TIP
When whisking egg whites, use a grease-free bowl and make sure that there are no traces of yolk.

Energy 446Kcal/1872kJ; Protein 10g; Carbohydrate 51g, of which sugars 43g; Fat 23g, of which saturates 21g; Cholesterol 283mg; Calcium 114mg; Fibre 0.4g; Sodium 270mg.

APPLE PUDDING

THIS IS ONE OF THE SIMPLEST AND YET MOST TASTY DESSERT RECIPES, MADE WITH APPLES FROM THE GARDEN AND ALL OTHER INGREDIENTS FROM THE STORE CUPBOARD. SLICED APPLES ARE SPREAD OUT IN A CAKE TIN AND TOPPED WITH A LIGHT SOUFFLÉ-LIKE SPONGE BEFORE BAKING.

SERVES 4

INGREDIENTS

    4 crisp eating apples
    a little lemon juice
    300ml/½ pint/1¼ cups milk
    40g/1½oz/3 tbsp butter
    40g/1½oz/⅓ cup plain (all-purpose)
      flour
    25g/1oz/2 tbsp caster (superfine) sugar
    2.5ml/½ tsp vanilla extract
    2 eggs, separated

1 Preheat the oven to 200°C/400°F/Gas 6. Butter a dish measuring 20–23cm/8–9in diameter and 5cm/2in deep. Peel, core and slice the apples, into the dish, and add the lemon juice.

2 Put the milk, butter and flour in a pan. Whisking continuously, cook over medium heat until the sauce thickens and comes to the boil. Let it bubble gently for 1–2 minutes, stirring to make sure it does not stick on the bottom. Pour into a bowl, add the sugar and vanilla, and then stir in the egg yolks.

3 In a separate bowl, whisk the egg whites until stiff peaks form. With a large metal spoon fold the egg whites into the custard. Pour the custard mixture over the apples in the dish.

4 Put into the hot oven and cook for about 40 minutes until firm to the touch. Serve straight out of the oven, before the topping begins to fall.

VARIATION
Stewed fruit, such as cooking apples, plums or rhubarb sweetened with honey or sugar, would also make a good base for this pudding, as would fresh summer berries (blackberries, raspberries, redcurrants and blackcurrants).
You could also use a layer of tinned pineapple if you don't have any fresh fruit to hand.

Energy 240kcal/1006kJ; Protein 7g; Carbohydrate 26.8g, of which sugars 19.2g; Fat 12.5g, of which saturates 6.8g; Cholesterol 121mg; Calcium 127mg; Fibre 1.9g; Sodium 131mg.

EVE'S PUDDING

THIS RECIPE WAS ORIGINALLY KNOWN AS 'MOTHER EVE'S PUDDING'. IT WOULD HAVE BEEN MADE WITH SUET PASTRY AND BOILED IN A BASIN COVERED WITH A CLOTH. THIS VERSION IS BAKED IN THE OVEN, AND IS MADE FROM A LIGHTER LEMON AND ALMOND-FLAVOURED SPONGE.

SERVES 4-6

INGREDIENTS

    115g/4oz/½ cup butter
    115g/4oz/½ cup caster (superfine)
      sugar
    2 eggs, beaten
    grated rind and juice of 1 lemon
    90g/3¼oz/scant 1 cup self-raising
      (self-rising) flour
    40g/1½oz/⅓ cup ground almonds
    115g/4oz/scant ½ cup soft light
      brown sugar
    550–675g/1¼–1½lb cooking apples,
      cored and thinly sliced
    25g/1oz/¼ cup flaked (sliced)
      almonds

1 Preheat the oven to 180°C/350°F/ Gas 4. Butter an ovenproof dish.

2 Beat together the butter and caster sugar in a large mixing bowl until the mixture is very light and fluffy.

3 Gradually beat the eggs into the butter mixture, beating well after each addition, then fold in the lemon rind, flour and ground almonds.

4 Mix the brown sugar, apples and lemon juice and tip the mixture into the ovenproof dish, spreading it out evenly.

5 Spoon the sponge mixture over the top and spread evenly. Sprinkle the almonds over. Bake for 40–45 minutes until risen and golden brown.

Energy 507kcal/2128kJ; Protein 6.9g; Carbohydrate 65.5g, of which sugars 52.7g; Fat 26.1g, of which saturates 12g; Cholesterol 114mg; Calcium 91mg; Fibre 2.8g; Sodium 159mg.

SUMMER PUDDING

NOTHING COULD BE MORE REDOLENT OF LATE SUMMER THAN THIS TRADITIONAL PUDDING. IT IS WONDERFULLY EASY TO MAKE, AND FRUGAL TOO, USING UP SLICES OF LEFTOVER BREAD AND WHATEVER SUMMER BERRIES AND OTHER FRUITS ARE AVAILABLE IN THE HEDGEROWS OR THE KITCHEN GARDEN.

SERVES 4-6

INGREDIENTS
8 x 1cm/½in thick slices of day-old
  white bread, crusts removed
800g/1¾lb/6–7 cups mixed berries,
  such as strawberries, raspberries,
  blackcurrants and redcurrants
50g/2oz/¼ cup golden caster
  (superfine) sugar
double (heavy) cream, to serve

1 Trim a slice of bread to fit in the base of a 1.2 litre/2 pint/5 cup bowl, then trim another 5–6 slices to line the sides of the bowl, making sure the bread comes up above the rim.

2 Place all the fruit in a pan with the sugar. Do not add any water. Cook gently for 4–5 minutes until the juices begin to run.

3 Allow the mixture to cool then spoon the berries, and enough of their juices to moisten, into the bread-lined bowl. Reserve any remaining juice to serve with the pudding.

4 Fold over the excess bread from the side of the bowl. Cover the fruit with the remaining bread, trimming to fit.

5 Place a small plate that fits inside the bowl on top of the pudding. Weight it down with a 900g/2lb weight, if you have one, or use a couple of full cans.

6 Chill the pudding in the refrigerator for at least 8 hours. To serve, run a knife between the pudding and the bowl and turn out on to a serving plate. Spoon any reserved juices over the top.

Energy 230kcal/977kJ; Protein 6.2g; Carbohydrate 51.7g, of which sugars 26.5g; Fat 1.2g, of which saturates 0g; Cholesterol 0mg; Calcium 98mg; Fibre 3g; Sodium 294mg.

BAKED CHEESECAKE

This is the traditional baked cheesecake, made with cottage or ricotta cheese studded with dried fruits. It is set on a lovely butter and breadcrumb base, and makes a light and delicious dessert, ideal for a summer picnic, or Sunday lunch in the garden.

SERVES 6–8

INGREDIENTS

 15g/½oz/1 tbsp butter
 45ml/3 tbsp fresh white breadcrumbs
 4 eggs
 100g/3¾oz mixed (candied) peel
 500g/1¼lb/2 cups cottage or
  ricotta cheese
 90g/3½oz/½ cup caster (superfine)
  sugar
 50g/2oz/scant ½ cup raisins
 grated rind of 1 lemon
 45ml/3 tbsp semolina
 icing (confectioners') sugar, for dusting
 crème fraîche or whipped cream, and
  fresh berries, to serve

1 Use the butter to grease the bottom and sides of a 20cm/8in loose-bottomed cake tin (pan). Pour in the breadcrumbs and tip and shake until the insides of the tin are well coated with the breadcrumbs.

2 Preheat the oven to 180°C/350°F/ Gas 4. Separate the egg yolks from the egg whites into two separate large bowls. Finely chop the candied peel and add to the egg yolks. Add the cottage or ricotta cheese, sugar, raisins, lemon rind and semolina and mix well.

3 Whisk the egg whites until they are stiff and hold their shape, then carefully fold into the cheese mixture. Spoon the mixture into the prepared tin.

4 Bake the cake in the oven for 30–40 minutes, until a skewer, inserted in the centre, comes out dry. Leave the cake to cool in the tin.

5 Slide a knife around the edge of the cake and carefully remove it from the tin. Place on a serving plate and dust with sifted icing sugar.

6 Serve with crème fraîche or whipped cream and fresh berries.

Energy 297kcal/1239kJ; Protein 7.6g; Carbohydrate 27.2g, of which sugars 19g; Fat 18g, of which saturates 9g; Cholesterol 83mg; Calcium 56mg; Fibre 1.1g; Sodium 139mg.

BAKED APPLES WITH MARZIPAN

THIS IS A TRADITIONAL RECIPE FOR THE WINTER, WHEN APPLES WERE ONCE THE ONLY FRESH FRUITS AVAILABLE AND COOKS NEEDED TO BE VERY CREATIVE TO FIND DIFFERENT WAYS TO SERVE THEM. THE BRANDY, RAISINS, NUTS AND MARZIPAN IN THE FILLING GIVE IT A REAL FLAVOUR OF CHRISTMAS.

SERVES 4

INGREDIENTS
5ml/1 tsp raisins
10ml/2 tsp brandy
4 large, crisp eating apples, such
   as Braeburn
75g/3oz marzipan, chopped
juice of ½ lemon
20g/¾oz/¼ cup chopped nuts
single (light) cream, to serve

VARIATION
You can vary the nuts in the recipe –
walnuts, hazelnuts and almonds, or even
pistachios, can be used.

1 Preheat the oven to 160°C/325°F/
Gas 3. Soak the raisins in the brandy
for 20 minutes.

2 Meanwhile, core the apples with a
corer or cut them out with a sharp
knife. Cut a small slice off the bottom of
each apple, if necessary, so that they
will stand up while they are cooking.
Score the skin around the apple in
three places to prevent it rolling up
during baking.

3 Mix the marzipan with the lemon
juice, chopped nuts, raisins and
brandy, and push the filling into the
centre of the apples. Put the apples on
a baking tray lined with baking
parchment, and bake them for 20–25
minutes. Serve the apples warm with
single cream.

Energy 150kcal/631kJ; Protein 2.2g; Carbohydrate 22.9g, of which sugars 22.7g; Fat 5.3g, of which saturates 0.6g; Cholesterol 0mg; Calcium 23mg; Fibre 2.3g; Sodium 33mg.

POACHED PEARS WITH CHOCOLATE

PEARS AND CHOCOLATE ARE ONE OF THE GREAT COMBINATIONS THAT COOKS HAVE KNOWN ABOUT FOR CENTURIES. THIS IS A VERY SIMPLE RECIPE FOR HALVED PEARS, SIMMERED WITH SUGAR AND TOPPED WITH HOME-MADE CHOCOLATE SAUCE, THEN SERVED WARM WITH ICE CREAM.

SERVES 4

INGREDIENTS

   4 firm dessert pears, peeled
   250g/9oz/1¼ cups caster (superfine)
     sugar
   600ml/1 pint/2½ cups water
   500ml/17fl oz/2¼ cups vanilla
     ice cream, to serve
For the chocolate sauce
   250g/9oz good quality dark
     (bittersweet) chocolate (minimum
     70 per cent cocoa solids)
   40g/1½oz unsalted butter
   5ml/1 tsp vanilla extract
   75ml/5 tbsp double (heavy) cream

1 Cut the pears in half lengthways and remove the core. Place the sugar and water in a large pan and gently heat until the sugar has dissolved.

2 Add the pear halves to the pan, then simmer for about 20 minutes, or until the pears are tender but not falling apart. Lift out of the sugar syrup with a slotted spoon and leave to cool.

3 To make the chocolate sauce, break the chocolate into small pieces and put into a pan. Add the butter and 30ml/ 2 tbsp water to the pan. Heat gently over a low heat, without stirring, until the chocolate has melted. Remove the pan from the heat.

4 Add the vanilla extract and cream to the melted chocolate, and mix gently.

5 When you are ready to serve, place a scoop of ice cream into each of four glasses. Add two cooled pear halves to each and pour over the hot chocolate sauce. Serve immediately.

Energy 1014kcal/4255kJ; Protein 8.8g; Carbohydrate 145.1g, of which sugars 143.2g; Fat 46.7g, of which saturates 29.6g; Cholesterol 81mg; Calcium 206mg; Fibre 4.9g; Sodium 152mg.

FRUIT AND WINE JELLY

IN 17TH-CENTURY ENGLAND, MAKING JELLY WAS A LENGTHY PROCESS THAT INVOLVED THE BOILING OF CALF'S HOOF, HARTSHORN OR ISINGLASS. NOW, THOUGH, GELATINE IS USED TO MAKE A LIGHT AND ELEGANT DESSERT. ALLOW PLENTY OF TIME FOR SIEVING THE FRUIT AND COOLING THE JELLY.

SERVES 6

INGREDIENTS
  600g/1lb 6oz fresh raspberries
  140g/5oz/¾ cup white sugar
  300ml/½ pint/1¼ cups medium-dry
    white wine
  5 leaves of gelatine (6 if the jelly
    is to be set in a mould and
    turned out)

GRANDMOTHER'S TIP
Instead of making your own fruit juice, use a carton of juice, such as mango, cranberry or orange, sweetened to taste.

1 Put the raspberries and sugar in a pan with 100ml/3½fl oz/scant ½ cup water and heat gently until the fruit releases its juices and becomes very soft, and the sugar has dissolved.

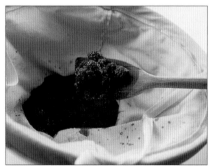

2 Remove the pan from the heat, pour the mixture into a fine nylon sieve (strainer) or jelly bag over a large bowl, and leave to strain – this will take some time, but do not squeeze the fruit or the resulting juice may be cloudy.

3 When the juice has drained into the bowl, make it up to 600ml/1 pint/2½ cups with water if necessary. Soften the gelatine in cold water for 5 minutes.

4 Heat half the juice until very hot but not quite boiling. Remove from the heat. Squeeze the softened gelatine to remove excess water, then stir it into the hot juice until dissolved. Add the remaining raspberry juice and the wine.

5 Pour into stemmed glasses and chill until set. Alternatively, set the jelly in a wetted mould and turn out onto a pretty plate for serving.

Energy 178kcal/758kJ; Protein 8.6g; Carbohydrate 29.3g, of which sugars 29.3g; Fat 0.3g, of which saturates 0.1g; Cholesterol 0mg; Calcium 42mg; Fibre 2.5g; Sodium 6mg.

SYLLABUS

THE ORIGINS OF THIS DISH CAN BE TRACED BACK AT LEAST AS FAR AS THE 17TH CENTURY. IT IS SAID TO HAVE BEEN MADE BY POURING MILK FRESH FROM THE COW ON TO SWEETENED, SPICED CIDER OR ALE. THIS MORE ADULT VERSION USES SHERRY AND CREAM FOR A GREAT CLASSIC DESSERT.

1 Finely grate 2.5ml/½ tsp rind from the orange, then squeeze out its juice.

2 Put the orange rind and juice, sugar and sherry into a large bowl and stir until the sugar is completely dissolved. Stir in the cream. Whip the mixture until it is thick and soft peaks form.

3 Carefully spoon the syllabub into wine glasses.

4 Chill the glasses of syllabub until ready to serve, then decorate with strips of crystallized orange.

SERVES 6

INGREDIENTS
   1 orange
   65g/2½oz/⅓ cup caster (superfine) sugar
   60ml/4 tbsp medium dry sherry
   300ml/½ pint/1½ cups double (heavy) cream
   crystallized orange, to decorate

GRANDMOTHER'S TIPS
• Syllabub is lovely spooned over a bowl of fresh soft fruit such as strawberries, apricots, raspberries or blackberries. You can also serve it with traditional sponge fingers, or thin crisp biscuits (cookies).
• Add a pinch of ground cinnamon to the mixture in step 2 if you are making this at Christmas time.

Energy 310kcal/1282kJ; Protein 1.1g; Carbohydrate 14.5g, of which sugars 14.5g; Fat 26.9g, of which saturates 16.7g; Cholesterol 69mg; Calcium 41mg; Fibre 0.3g; Sodium 15mg.

GOOSEBERRY FOOL

This quickly made, simple dessert never fails to impress. The basic recipe works well with any garden fruit, such as raspberries, rhubarb or blackcurrants. Adjust the sweetness to suit the fruit — for instance, gooseberries will need more sugar than raspberries.

SERVES 4

INGREDIENTS

    450g/1lb gooseberries, cut into half
      or chopped
    125g/4½oz/¼ cup caster (superfine)
      sugar, or to taste
    300ml/½ pint/1¼ cups double
      (heavy) cream
    sweet biscuits, to serve

1 Put the gooseberries into a pan with 30ml/2 tbsp water. Cover and cook gently for about 10 minutes until the fruit is soft. Stir in the sugar to taste.

2 Pour the fruit into a sieve (strainer) and press through. Leave to cool.

3 Whip the cream until stiff enough to hold soft peaks. Stir in the gooseberry purée without over-mixing (it looks pretty with some streaks).

4 Spoon the mixture into serving glasses and refrigerate until required.

Energy 517kcal/2147kJ; Protein 2.6g; Carbohydrate 37.3g, of which sugars 37.3g; Fat 40.7g, of which saturates 25.1g; Cholesterol 103mg; Calcium 85mg; Fibre 2.7g; Sodium 21mg.

RASPBERRY TRIFLE

This is the recipe that best sums up childhood. It is ideal for using up cake that is past its best, mixed with jam from the larder and seasonal soft fruit from the garden. There is also the addition of a little sherry to tempt the grown-ups.

SERVES 6 OR MORE

INGREDIENTS
  6oz (170g) trifle sponges, or
    1in (2.5cm) cubes of plain Victoria
    sponge, or coarsely crumbled
    sponge fingers
  4 tablespoons medium sherry
  4oz (115g) raspberry jam
  10oz (300g) raspberries
  ¾ pint (450ml) custard, flavoured
    with 2 tablespoons medium or sweet
    sherry (optional)
  ½ pint (300ml) double (heavy)
    cream, whipped
  toasted flaked almonds and mint
    leaves, to decorate

VARIATIONS
Try other fruit in the trifle, with a jam and liqueur flavour to suit: apricots, peaches, nectarines, strawberries, etc. Another traditional cake to use in a trifle is Swiss roll (jelly roll). If you are serving the trifle to children, use fruit juice instead of sherry to moisten the cake.

1 Spread half of the sponges, cake cubes or sponge fingers over the bottom of a large serving bowl. (A glass bowl is best for presentation.)

2 Sprinkle half of the sherry over the cake to moisten it. Spoon over half of the jam, dotting it evenly over the cake.

3 Reserve a few raspberries for decoration. Make a layer of half of the remaining raspberries on top.

4 Pour over half of the custard, covering the fruit and cake. Repeat the layers. Cover and chill in the refrigerator for at least 2 hours.

5 Before serving, spoon the whipped cream evenly over the top. To decorate, sprinkle the trifle with toasted flaked almonds and arrange the reserved raspberries and the mint leaves on the top.

Energy 330Kcal/1382kJ; Protein 5.1g; Carbohydrate 35.9g, of which sugars 29.1g; Fat 17.7g, of which saturates 9.9g; Cholesterol 90mg; Calcium 102mg; Fibre 1.1g; Sodium 59mg.

STRAWBERRY SNOW

STRAWBERRIES HAVE A DELICATE, FRAGRANT TASTE AND TEXTURE, AND MOST DESSERTS MADE FROM CHOPPED OR CRUSHED STRAWBERRIES ARE BEST EATEN AS SOON AS POSSIBLE AFTER THEY ARE MADE. THIS IS AN IDEAL FAMILY PUDDING, OR AN AFTERNOON TREAT, TO EAT IN SUMMER.

SERVES 4

INGREDIENTS
   120ml/4fl oz/½ cup water
   15ml/1 tbsp powdered gelatine
   300g/11oz/2¾ cups strawberries,
    lightly crushed
   250ml/8fl oz/1 cup double
    (heavy) cream
   4 egg whites
   90g/3½oz/½ cup caster (superfine)
    sugar
   halved strawberries, to decorate

1 Put the water in a heatproof bowl and sprinkle in the gelatine. Stand the bowl over a pan of hot water and heat gently until dissolved. Remove the bowl from the pan and leave to cool slightly.

2 Put half the crushed strawberries in a pan and bring to the boil.

3 Remove from the heat, then stir in the dissolved gelatine. Chill the mixture in the refrigerator for about 2 hours until it has a syrupy consistency.

4 Pour the cream into a bowl and whisk until it holds its shape. Set it aside while you prepare the egg whites.

5 In a large, clean bowl, whisk the egg whites until stiff, gradually adding the sugar as they rise. Fold the egg whites into the cream and strawberry mixture, then fold in the remaining crushed strawberries, followed by the whipped cream.

6 Turn the mixture into individual serving dishes and serve immediately, or chill until required. Serve, decorated with halved strawberries.

GRANDMOTHER'S TIP
Strawberry Snow freezes well and can then be served in slices. All you have to do is spoon the mixture into a loaf tin (pan) lined with clear film (plastic wrap) and freeze for a couple of hours, until it is firm, slice and serve.

Energy 443kcal/1841kJ; Protein 7.8g; Carbohydrate 29.1g, of which sugars 29.1g; Fat 33.7g, of which saturates 20.9g; Cholesterol 86mg; Calcium 56mg; Fibre 0.8g; Sodium 81mg.

CHOCOLATE <u>AND</u> COFFEE MOUSSE

A LIGHT CHOCOLATE MOUSSE IS ALWAYS A POPULAR WAY TO END A MEAL. THIS INDULGENT VERSION IS MADE WITH A GOOD STRONG CHOCOLATE FLAVOURED WITH COFFEE AND RUM. BRANDY OR VODKA COULD ALSO BE USED. YOU CAN OMIT THE COFFEE OR ALCOHOL, DEPENDING ON YOUR PREFERENCE.

SERVES 4–6

INGREDIENTS
- 250g/9oz dark (bittersweet) chocolate (minimum 70 per cent cocoa solids)
- 60ml/4 tbsp cooled strong black coffee
- 8 eggs, separated
- 200g/7oz/1 cup caster (superfine) sugar
- 60ml/4 tbsp rum, brandy or vodka (optional)

1 Break the chocolate into small pieces and melt in a heatproof bowl over a pan of gently simmering water. Ensure the water does not touch the base of the bowl, or the chocolate may seize and crystallize.

2 Once the chocolate has completely melted, stir in the cold coffee. Leave to cool slightly.

3 Beat the egg yolks with half the sugar until it is pale, thick and creamy. Add the rum, brandy or vodka and stir in the melted chocolate mixture.

4 Whisk the egg whites in a separate bowl until stiff peaks form.

5 Stir in the remaining sugar, then fold into the chocolate mixture. Spoon into chilled glasses or ramekins. Chill the mousse for at least an hour before serving.

Energy 464kcal/1951kJ; Protein 10.6g; Carbohydrate 61.3g, of which sugars 60.9g; Fat 19.1g, of which saturates 9.1g; Cholesterol 256mg; Calcium 70mg; Fibre 1.1g; Sodium 98mg.

APPLE SNOW

THIS COMFORTING NURSERY DISH IS AS SIMPLE AS IT IS DELICIOUS — AND IS BEST MADE WITH LATE-CROPPING COOKING APPLES, HARVESTED IN THE AUTUMN. THEY 'FALL' (DON'T HOLD THEIR SHAPE) WHEN COOKED, AND MAKE A FLUFFY PURÉE. SERVE WITH CRISP COOKIES, OR SPONGE FINGERS.

SERVES 6

INGREDIENTS
675g/1½lb cooking apples
a little thinly peeled lemon rind
about 115g/4oz/generous ½ cup
  caster (superfine) sugar
3 egg whites

1 Peel, core and slice the apples. Turn into a pan with 45ml/3 tbsp water and the lemon rind.

2 Cover and simmer gently for 15 minutes, until the apples break down.

3 Remove the pan from the heat, take out the lemon rind, and sweeten to taste with caster sugar.

4 Beat the apples well with a wooden spoon to make a purée, or rub through a sieve if a smoother texture is preferred. Leave to cool.

5 When the purée is cold, whisk the egg whites until stiff.

6 Fold the egg whites into the apple using a metal spoon. Whisk together until the mixture is thick and light.

7 Turn into a serving bowl, or divide between six individual dishes, and chill until required.

Energy 121Kcal/516kJ; Protein 1.8g; Carbohydrate 30.1g, of which sugars 30.1g; Fat 0.1g, of which saturates 0g; Cholesterol 0mg; Calcium 7mg; Fibre 1.8g; Sodium 34mg.

CAKES AND BREADS

*There are hundreds of classic recipes for cakes
and breads that have been passed down to us by
previous generations of cooks. From the lightest,
airiest sponge cake, suitable for serving for
afternoon tea, to a rustic tea bread, packed with
fruit, that will keep you going for a hard
afternoon's gardening or walking the dog, there
is something in this chapter for everyone.*

VANILLA SPONGE WITH STRAWBERRIES

THIS SPONGE CAKE IS FAT-FREE AND IDEAL TO MAKE FOR A SUMMER TEA, FILLED WITH FRESH SOFT FRUIT. THE CLASSIC NAME FOR THE CAKE IS 'GENOESE', AND IT BECAME POPULAR IN THE 1800s. IT HELPS TO HAVE ALL THE INGREDIENTS READY AT ROOM TEMPERATURE.

SERVES 8–10

INGREDIENTS
    white vegetable fat (shortening),
        for greasing
    115g/4oz/generous ½ cup caster
        (superfine) sugar, plus extra for
        dusting
    90g/3½oz/¾ cup plain (all-purpose)
        flour, sifted, plus extra for dusting
    4 eggs
    icing (confectioners') sugar, for
        dusting
For the filling
    300ml/½ pint/1¼ cups double (heavy)
        cream
    about 5ml/1 tsp icing (confectioners')
        sugar, sieved
    450g/1lb/4 cups strawberries,
        washed and hulled
    a little Cointreau, or other fruit
        liqueur (optional)

GRANDMOTHER'S TIPS
• Like all fatless sponges, this cake is best eaten on the day of baking.
• One trick for a lighter cake is to whisk the sponge mixture over hot water to help make it rise.

1 Preheat the oven to 190°C/375°F/ Gas 5. Grease a loose-based 20cm/ 8in deep cake tin (pan) with white vegetable fat, and dust it with 5ml/1 tsp caster sugar mixed with 5ml/1 tsp flour. Shake off any excess sugar and flour mixture and discard.

2 Put the eggs and sugar into the bowl of an electric mixer and whisk at high speed until it is light and thick, and the mixture leaves a trail as it drops from the whisk. Alternatively, whisk by hand, or with a hand-held electric whisk; set the bowl over a pan one quarter filled with hot water and whisk until thick and creamy, then remove from the heat.

3 Sift the flour evenly over the whisked eggs and carefully fold it in with a metal spoon, mixing thoroughly but losing as little volume as possible.

4 Pour the mixture into the prepared cake tin. Shake gently to level off the top and bake in the preheated oven for 25–30 minutes, or until the sponge feels springy to the touch.

5 Leave in the tin for 1–2 minutes to allow the cake to cool a little and shrink slightly from the sides, then loosen the sides gently with a knife and turn out on to a rack to cool.

6 When the sponge is cold, make the filling. Whip the double cream with a little icing sugar until it is stiff enough to hold its shape. Slice the sponge across the middle with a sharp knife and divide half of the cream between the two inner sides of the cake.

7 Select some well-shaped even-sized strawberries for the top of the cake, and then slice the rest.

8 Lay the bottom half of the sponge on a serving plate and arrange the sliced strawberries on the cream. Sprinkle with liqueur, if using. Cover with the second half of the cake and press down gently so that it holds together.

9 Spread the remaining cream on top of the cake, and arrange the reserved strawberries, whole or halved according to size, on top.

10 Set aside for an hour or so for the flavours to develop, then dust lightly with icing sugar and serve as a dessert.

VARIATION
For raspberry sponge, halve the amount of cream in the recipe, omit the strawberries and replace with raspberry jam. After halving the cake, whip the cream to form soft peaks. Spread the bottom half of the cake with jam. Cover with cream, put the second half of the cake on top and dust with icing sugar. Leave in the refrigerator, or in a cool place, for 1 hour before serving.

Energy 333Kcal/1387kJ; Protein 5.3g; Carbohydrate 27.8g, of which sugars 19.2g; Fat 23.1g, of which saturates 13.3g; Cholesterol 147mg; Calcium 65mg; Fibre 1g; Sodium 48mg.

CHERRY CAKE

BOTH DRIED AND GLACÉ CHERRIES ARE USED IN THIS CAKE, PARTNERED WITH THE DELICATE FLAVOUR OF ALMONDS AND DECORATED WITH A DRIZZLE OF ICING. IT IS A COMBINATION THAT IS PERFECT FOR A SUMMER TEA PARTY ON THE LAWN WHEN FRIENDS OR FAMILY COME TO CALL.

SERVES 10

INGREDIENTS
- 175g/6oz/¾ cup unsalted butter, softened, plus extra for greasing
- 175g/6oz/scant 1 cup caster (superfine) sugar
- 3 eggs, beaten
- 150g/5oz/1¼ cups self-raising (self-rising) flour
- 50g/2oz/½ cup plain (all-purpose) flour
- 75g/3oz/¾ cup ground almonds
- 75g/3oz/scant ½ cup glacé (candied) cherries, washed, dried and halved
- 25g/1oz dried cherries
- a few drops of almond extract

For the decoration
- 115g/4oz/1 cup icing (confectioners') sugar, sifted
- 5ml/1 tsp lemon juice
- 50g/2oz/½ cup flaked (sliced) almonds, toasted
- 10 natural glacé (candied) cherries

1 Preheat the oven to 160°C/325°F/Gas 3. Grease and line a 20cm/8in round deep cake tin (pan).

2 In a bowl, beat the butter with the sugar until light and fluffy, using an electric whisk, if possible. Add the eggs a little at a time, including 5ml/1 tsp of flour with each addition.

3 Sift the flour into the bowl, together with the ground almonds and both types of cherries and fold into the butter and sugar mixture until smooth.

4 Stir the almond extract into the mixture, then spoon into the cake tin and smooth level.

5 Bake for 45–50 minutes, or until a skewer inserted into the centre comes out clean. Cool slightly, then turn on to a wire rack to go cold. Remove the lining paper.

6 In a bowl, mix the icing sugar with the lemon juice, and 10–15ml/2–3 tsp water, to make a soft icing.

7 Drizzle half the icing over the cake. Sprinkle the almonds in the centre. Place the cherries around the edge and drizzle over the remaining icing.

Energy 367kcal/1535kJ; Protein 5g; Carbohydrate 43.7g, of which sugars 26.6g; Fat 20.4g, of which saturates 12g; Cholesterol 118mg; Calcium 75mg; Fibre 0.9g; Sodium 309mg.

LEMON DRIZZLE CAKE

THIS CLASSIC RECIPE IS A FAVOURITE AT COFFEE MORNINGS, FOR A TEATIME SNACK OR A SUPPERTIME TREAT. THE WONDERFULLY MOIST CAKE IS TRANSFORMED INTO SOMETHING SPECIAL BY POURING LEMON AND SUGAR SYRUP OVER THE COOKED SPONGE WHILE IT IS STILL WARM FROM THE OVEN.

SERVES 6

INGREDIENTS
  225g/8oz/1 cup unsalted butter,
    softened, plus extra for greasing
  finely grated rind of 2 lemons
  175g/6oz/scant 1 cup caster
    (superfine) sugar, plus 5ml/1 tsp
  4 eggs
  225g/8oz/2 cups self-raising
    (self-rising) flour, sifted with 5ml/
    1 tsp baking powder
  grated rind of 1 lemon,
    to decorate
For the syrup
  juice of 1 lemon
  150g/5oz/¾ cup caster
    (superfine) sugar

1 Preheat the oven to 160°C/325°F/ Gas 3. Grease and line an 18–20cm/ 7–8in round deep cake tin (pan) with baking parchment so the paper is higher than the sides of the tin.

2 Mix the lemon rind and sugar together in a bowl.

3 In a large bowl, beat the butter with the lemon and sugar mixture until light and fluffy, then beat in the eggs one at a time. Sift the flour and baking powder into the mixture in three batches and beat well.

GRANDMOTHER'S TIPS
Leaving the cake in the tin to cool means that all of the delicious lemon syrup soaks into the cake.

4 Turn the batter into the prepared tin and smooth the top level. Bake for 1½ hours, or until golden brown and springy to the touch.

5 To make the syrup, slowly heat the juice with the sugar until dissolved.

6 Prick the cake top with a skewer and pour over the syrup, then leave to cool. When completely cool, take the cake out of the tin. Remove the lining paper, then sprinkle over the grated lemon rind together with 5ml/1 tsp sugar, and slice to serve.

Energy 659kcal/2765kJ; Protein 8g; Carbohydrate 84.1g, of which sugars 56.2g; Fat 34.8g, of which saturates 21.4g; Cholesterol 213mg; Calcium 184mg; Fibre 1.2g; Sodium 466mg.

ICED WALNUT LAYER CAKE

MANY A VILLAGE TEA ROOM FEATURES THIS TRADITIONAL CAKE ON A PRETTY STAND. THE CHOPPED WALNUTS IN THE SPONGE MIXTURE BLEND WELL WITH THE BUTTERCREAM FILLING, AND HALVED NUTS MAKE A LOVELY DECORATION ON TOP OF THE SWIRLED FROSTING. IT KEEPS WELL IN AN AIRTIGHT TIN.

SERVES 12

INGREDIENTS
   225g/8oz/1 cup butter, softened, plus
      extra for greasing
   225g/8oz/2 cups self-raising (self-
      rising) flour
   5ml/1 tsp baking powder
   225g/8oz/1 cup soft light brown sugar
   75g/3oz/¾ cup walnuts, finely
      chopped
   4 eggs
   15ml/1 tbsp treacle (molasses)
For the buttercream
   75g/3oz/6 tbsp unsalted butter
   5ml/1 tsp vanilla extract
   175g/6oz/1½ cups icing
      (confectioners') sugar
For the meringue frosting
   2 large (US extra large) egg whites
   350g/12oz/1¾ cups golden caster
      (superfine) sugar
   pinch of salt
   pinch of cream of tartar
   15ml/1 tbsp warm water
   whole walnut halves, to decorate

1 Preheat the oven to 160°C/325°F/
Gas 3. Grease and line two 20cm/8in
round shallow cake tins (pans) with
baking parchment.

2 Sift the flour and baking powder into
a large bowl, then add all the remaining
ingredients. Beat vigorously for 2
minutes until smooth, then divide the
mixture between the tins and spread
level. Bake for 25 minutes until golden
and springy to the touch in the centre.

3 Allow the tins to stand for 5 minutes,
then turn the cakes out on to a wire
rack to cool. Remove the lining papers.
Cut each cake in half horizontally using
a long-bladed sharp knife.

4 Meanwhile make the buttercream.
Beat the butter, vanilla extract and icing
sugar together until light and fluffy.
Spread a third thinly over one sponge
half and place a sponge layer on top.

5 Continue layering the other 3 halves
of sponge cakes with the buttercream.
Then transfer the cake on to a plate.

6 To make the frosting, put the
egg whites in a large heatproof bowl
and add the caster sugar, salt, cream of
tartar and water. Put the bowl over a
pan of hot water and whisk with an
electric mixer for 7 minutes, or until the
mixture is thick and stands in peaks.

7 Immediately, use a metal spatula to
swirl the frosting over the top and sides
of the cake.

8 Arrange the walnut halves on top of
the cake and leave it to set for at least
10 minutes before serving.

CHOCOLATE CAKE WITH COFFEE ICING

THIS IS AN EASY ALL-IN-ONE VERSION OF A TRADITIONAL FAMILY FAVOURITE. IT CAN BE DECORATED WITH SWIRLS OF ICING AND WHOLE NUTS TO MAKE A BIRTHDAY CAKE OR FOR ANY SPECIAL OCCASION. THE COFFEE ICING BEAUTIFULLY COMPLEMENTS THE RICH CHOCOLATE FLAVOUR OF THE CAKE.

MAKES AN 18CM/7IN CAKE

INGREDIENTS
    175g/6oz/1½ cups self-raising (self-
    rising) flour
    25ml/1½ tbsp unsweetened cocoa
    powder
    pinch of salt
    175g/6oz/¾ cup butter, softened, or
    soft margarine
    175g/6oz/¾ cup soft dark brown
    sugar
    50g/2oz/½ cup ground almonds
    3 large (US extra large) eggs,
    lightly beaten
For the coffee butter icing
    175g/6oz/¾ cup unsalted butter, at
    warm room temperature
    350g/12oz/3 cups sifted icing
    (confectioners') sugar
    30ml/2 tbsp coffee essence (extract)
    whole hazelnuts or pecan nuts, to
    decorate (optional)

VARIATION
For a deliciously rich touch, 15–30ml/ 1–2 tbsp of coffee liqueur can be included in the icing – beat in with the coffee essence at the end of step 4.

1 Preheat the oven to 180°C/350°F/ Gas 4 and butter two 18cm/7in diameter sandwich tins (pans).

2 Sift the flour, cocoa and salt into a mixing bowl. Cut in the butter or margarine and add the sugar, ground almonds and eggs.

3 Mix with a wooden spoon for 2–3 minutes, until thoroughly mixed; the mixture should be smooth, with no traces of butter remaining.

4 Divide the mixture between the prepared tins and bake in the centre of the preheated oven for 25–30 minutes, or until springy to the touch. Turn the cakes out and cool on a wire rack.

5 Meanwhile, make the icing: cream the butter well in a large bowl, then gradually beat in the sifted icing sugar and the coffee essence.

6 When the cakes are cold, sandwich them together with some of the icing and cover the top and sides with most of the remainder. Pipe the remaining icing around the top in rosettes, if you like, and decorate with whole hazelnuts or pecan nuts.

Per cake: Energy 5899Kcal/24,684kJ; Protein 56.2g; Carbohydrate 691.1g, of which sugars 556.9g; Fat 343.1g, of which saturates 193.7g; Cholesterol 1.43g; Calcium 1.06g; Fibre 12.2g; Sodium 3.28g.

BOILED FRUIT CAKE

THE TEXTURE OF THIS FRUIT CAKE IS REALLY SPECIAL, WITH PLUMP DRIED FRUIT MADE EVEN MORE SUCCULENT BY HEATING IT GENTLY WITH THE BUTTER, SUGAR AND MILK BEFORE BAKING. THE IDEA ORIGINALLY COMES FROM WALES, WHICH HAS A LONG TRADITION OF DELICIOUS FRUIT CAKE RECIPES.

2 Put the dried fruit in a large pan and add the butter and sugar. Bring slowly to boil, stirring occasionally.

3 When the butter has melted and the sugar has dissolved, bubble the mixture gently for about 2 minutes. Remove from the heat and cool slightly.

4 Sift the flour with the bicarbonate of soda and mixed spice. Add this, this milk and the eggs to the fruit mixture and mix together well.

5 Pour the mixture into the prepared tin and smooth the surface.

6 Bake for about 1½ hours or until firm to the touch and the cake is cooked through – a skewer inserted in the centre should come out free of sticky mixture.

7 Leave in the tin to cool for 20–30 minutes, then turn out and cool completely on a wire rack.

MAKES A 20CM/8IN CAKE

INGREDIENTS
  350g/12oz/2 cups mixed dried fruit
  225g/8oz/1 cup butter
  225g/8oz/1 cup soft dark brown
    sugar
  400ml/14fl oz/1⅔ cup milk
  450g/1lb/4 cups self-raising (self-
    rising) flour
  5ml/1 tsp bicarbonate of soda
    (baking soda)
  5ml/1 tsp mixed (apple pie) spice
  2 eggs, beaten

1 Preheat the oven to 160°C/325°F/ Gas 3. Butter a 20cm/8in cake tin (pan) and line it with baking parchment.

Per cake: Energy 5150kcal/21689kJ; Protein 72.2g; Carbohydrate 796g, of which sugars 498.8g; Fat 209.1g, of which saturates 125.4g; Cholesterol 884mg; Calcium 2352mg; Fibre 20.1g; Sodium 3297mg.

OLD-FASHIONED TREACLE CAKE

THIS IS A GOOD HEARTY CAKE WHICH IS RELATIVELY QUICK TO MAKE. THE TREACLE ADDS EXTRA COLOUR AND FLAVOUR. IT WOULD BE AN IDEAL TREAT FOR HUNGRY CHILDREN AFTER SCHOOL, OR FOR SUSTAINING EVERYONE IN THE FAMILY ON A WALK THROUGH THE COUNTRYSIDE.

MAKES A 20cm/8in CAKE

INGREDIENTS
  250g/9oz/2 cups self-raising
    (self-rising) flour
  2.5ml/½ tsp mixed (apple pie)
    spice
  75g/3oz/6 tbsp butter, cut into
    small dice
  35g/1oz/2 tbsp caster
    (superfine) sugar
  150g/5oz/1 cup mixed
    dried fruit
  1 egg
  15ml/1 tbsp treacle (molasses)
  100ml/3½fl oz/scant ½ cup milk

3 Beat the egg and, with a small whisk or a fork, stir in the treacle and then the milk; add a little extra milk if necessary.

4 Transfer the cake mixture to the prepared dish or tin with a spoon and level out the surface.

5 Bake the cake in the hot oven and cook for about 1 hour until it has risen, is firm to the touch and fully cooked through. To check if the cake is cooked, insert a small skewer in the centre – it should come out free of sticky mixture.

6 Leave the cooked treacle cake to cool completely. Serve, cut into wedges, straight from the dish.

1 Preheat the oven to 180°C/350°F/ Gas 5. Butter a shallow 20–23cm/ 8–9in ovenproof flan dish (pan) or baking tin (pan).

2 Sift the flour and spice into a large mixing bowl. Add the butter and, with your fingertips, rub it into the flour until the mixture resembles fine crumbs. Alternatively, you could make this in a food processor. Stir in the sugar and mixed dried fruit.

GRANDMOTHER'S TIP
You can vary the fruit for this cake, depending on what you have in the storecupboard. Try using chopped ready-to-eat dried apricots and preserved stem ginger, or a packet of luxury dried fruit.

Per cake: Energy 2089kcal/8805kJ; Protein 37.4g; Carbohydrate 343g, of which sugars 152.4g; Fat 72.8g, of which saturates 42.2g; Cholesterol 356mg; Calcium 720mg; Fibre 11.1g; Sodium 676mg.

CHOCOLATE GINGER CRUNCH CAKE

THIS IS ONE OF THE EASIEST CAKES TO MAKE. IT IS A PERFECT RECIPE FOR CHILDREN TO COOK THEMSELVES WITH A LITTLE SUPERVISION — THEY WILL ENJOY BREAKING UP THE BISCUITS WITH A ROLLING PIN AND STIRRING THE MELTING CHOCOLATE. THE CHOPPED GINGER ADDS A SPICY TOUCH.

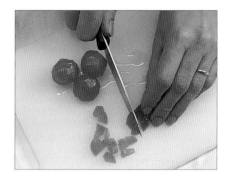

3 Chop the stem ginger fairly finely and mix with the crushed biscuits.

4 Stir the biscuit mixture, ginger syrup and coconut into the melted chocolate and butter, mixing well until combined.

5 Tip the mixture into the prepared flan ring and press down firmly and evenly.

6 Chill in the fridge until set. Remove the flan ring and slide the cake on to a plate. Melt the milk chocolate, drizzle it over the top and decorate with the pieces of crystallized ginger.

SERVES 6

INGREDIENTS
   150g/5oz plain (unsweetened)
     chocolate, broken into squares
   50g/2oz/4 tbsp unsalted butter
   115g/4oz ginger nut biscuits
     (gingersnaps)
   4 pieces preserved stem ginger
   30ml/2 tbsp stem ginger syrup
   45ml/3 tbsp desiccated (dry
     unsweetened) coconut
To decorate
   25g/1oz milk chocolate
   pieces of crystallized ginger

1 Crush the biscuits into small pieces and tip into a bowl.

2 Grease a 15cm/6in loose-bottomed flan ring (tart pan); and place it on a sheet of non-stick baking paper. Melt the plain chocolate with the butter in a heatproof bowl over simmering water. When melted, remove from the heat.

GRANDMOTHER'S TIP
Do not process the biscuits, as you need some crunchy pieces for texture. Put them in a stout plastic bag and crush them with a rolling pin.

Energy 340Kcal/1420kJ; Protein 3.1g; Carbohydrate 33.9g, of which sugars 25.4g; Fat 22.3g, of which saturates 14.5g; Cholesterol 20mg; Calcium 46mg; Fibre 2g; Sodium 121mg.

IRISH WHISKEY CAKE

*THIS IS A GROWN-UP CAKE FOR THOSE WHO LOVE THE EARTHY, STRONG FLAVOUR OF IRISH WHISKEY.
IT HAS ALL THE FLAVOUR OF LEMON AND SPICY CLOVES, WITH PLENTY OF SUCCULENT SULTANAS
SOAKED OVERNIGHT. A DRIZZLE OF LEMON-FLAVOURED ICING ON TOP ADDS THE FINISHING TOUCH.*

MAKES AN 18CM/7IN CAKE

INGREDIENTS
 225g/8oz/1⅓ cups sultanas (golden
  raisins)
 grated rind of 1 lemon
 150ml/¼ pint/⅔ cup Irish whiskey
 175g/6oz/¾ cup butter, softened
 175g/6oz/¾ cup soft light brown
  sugar
 175g/6oz/1½ cups plain
  (all-purpose) flour
 pinch of salt
 1.5ml/¼ tsp ground cloves
 5ml/1 tsp baking powder
 3 large (US extra large) eggs,
  separated
For the icing
 juice of 1 lemon
 225g/8oz/2 cups icing
  (confectioners') sugar
 crystallized lemon slices, to decorate
  (optional)

1 Put the sultanas and grated lemon
rind into a bowl with the whiskey and
leave overnight to soak.

2 Preheat the oven to 180°C/350°F/
Gas 4. Grease a loose-bottomed
18cm/7in deep cake tin (pan), and line
the base with baking parchment.

3 Cream the butter and sugar until
light and fluffy. Sift the flour, salt, cloves
and baking powder together into a bowl.

4 Beat the yolks into the butter and
sugar one at a time, adding a little of
the flour with each egg and beating well
after each addition.

5 Gradually blend in the sultana and
whiskey mixture, alternating with the
remaining flour. Do not overbeat.

GRANDMOTHER'S TIP
For an additional whiskey flavour you
could add a shot to the icing before you
mix in the water.

6 Whisk the egg whites until stiff and
fold them into the mixture with a metal
spoon. Turn the mixture into the
prepared tin and bake in the preheated
oven for 1½ hours, or until well risen
and springy to the touch. Turn the cake
out of the tin, and leave to cool
completely on a rack.

7 To make the icing, mix the lemon
juice with the sieved icing sugar and
enough warm water to make a pouring
consistency. Lay a plate under the cake
rack and slowly pour the icing over the
cake. Scoop up and reuse any icing
dripping on to the plate. When the icing
has set, decorate with lemon slices.

Per cake: Energy 4691Kcal/19,730kJ; Protein 48.1g; Carbohydrate 711.2g, of which sugars 577.8g; Fat 167g, of which saturates 97.1g; Cholesterol 1.06g; Calcium 735mg; Fibre 9.9g; Sodium 1.38g.

COUNTRY-STYLE APPLE TART

THIS CLASSIC APPLE TART IS PACKED WITH FRUIT AND FLAVOURED WITH CINNAMON. THE CRUST RESEMBLES A CAKE MIXTURE, RATHER THAN PASTRY, WHICH GIVES A WONDERFULLY LIGHT RESULT. EATING APPLES RATHER THAN COOKING APPLES ARE USED FOR ADDED SWEETNESS.

SERVES 6

INGREDIENTS
  215g/7½oz/scant 2 cups plain (all-purpose) flour, plus extra for rolling
  5ml/1 tsp baking powder
  pinch of salt
  115g/4oz/½ cup cold unsalted butter, cubed
  finely grated rind of ½ lemon
  75g/3oz/scant ½ cup caster (superfine) sugar, plus extra for sprinkling
  2 small (US medium) eggs
  3 eating apples, peeled and cubed
  ground cinnamon
  whipped cream, to serve

1 Sift the flour, baking powder and salt into a food processor. Add the butter and grated lemon rind and process briefly to combine, then add the sugar, 1 whole egg and the yolk of the second egg to the flour mixture, and process to make a soft dough.

2 Divide the dough into two pieces, one portion nearly double the size of the other. Wrap in clear film (plastic wrap) and chill for at least 2 hours until firm.

3 Preheat the oven to 180°C/350°F/ Gas 4. Place a baking sheet in the oven and grease a 20cm/8in loose-bottomed flan tin (tart pan).

4 Place the larger piece of dough on a lightly floured piece of clear film (plastic wrap) and cover with another piece of film. Roll out to a 25cm/10in round. Remove the film and place the dough in the tin. Press into the tin so that it stands just clear of the top.

5 Pack the tin with the apples and sprinkle with cinnamon. Roll out the second piece of dough in the same way, to exactly the same size as the tin. Lay the dough on top of the apples and fold the overlapping edges of the bottom piece of dough inward. Gently press the edges together with a fork, to seal.

6 Prick the dough a few times, brush with egg white and sprinkle with sugar. Place on the hot baking sheet and bake for 20 minutes, then reduce the temperature to 160°C/325°F/Gas 3 for a further 25–30 minutes until golden.

7 Leave the tart to cool in the tin for 30 minutes, then unmould and cool on a wire rack. Serve with whipped cream.

Energy 232Kcal/984kJ; Protein 5.7g; Carbohydrate 45.4g, of which sugars 18.1g; Fat 4.4g, of which saturates 1.9g; Cholesterol 69mg; Calcium 69mg; Fibre 1.9g; Sodium 41mg.

SWISS ROLL

ROLLED SPONGE CAKE IS A NURSERY TREAT THAT IS NOT DIFFICULT TO MAKE IF YOU FOLLOW THE INSTRUCTIONS BELOW. THIS ONE IS FILLED WITH CHOCOLATE BUTTERCREAM, BUT A FRUITY JAM AND SOME FRESHLY CHOPPED BERRIES SUCH AS STRAWBERRIES OR RASPBERRIES WOULD TASTE DELICIOUS.

SERVES 12

INGREDIENTS
   50g/2oz/½ cup self-raising (self-rising) flour
   25g/1oz/¼ cup cornflour
   5ml/1 tsp baking powder
   3 eggs
   250g/9oz/1¼ cups caster (superfine) sugar
   30ml/2 tbsp water
For the chocolate buttercream filling
   50g/2oz/¼ cup unsalted butter
   90g/3oz/⅔ cup icing (confectioner's) sugar, sifted
   1 egg yolk
   30ml/2tbsp unsweetened cocoa powder, sifted, plus extra for dusting

1 Preheat the oven to 190°C/375°F/Gas 5. Lightly grease a 27 x 38cm/10½ x 15in Swiss roll tin (jelly roll pan). Line with baking parchment and lightly grease it.

2 Sift together the cornflour, flour and baking powder in a mixing bowl. Whisk the eggs and 150g/5oz/¾ cup of the sugar together in a separate bowl until light and foamy.

3 Gradually fold the flour into the egg mixture, continuing to beat until smooth. Add the water. Spread the batter evenly over the prepared tin and bake for 10–12 minutes until golden brown. Sprinkle a clean dish towel with the remaining sugar.

4 To make the chocolate buttercream filling, cream the butter and icing sugar in a large bowl until light and fluffy.

5 Stir in the egg yolk until blended, add the cocoa and mix thoroughly.

GRANDMOTHER'S TIP
Don't let the cake cool flat, otherwise it will crack and break when you roll it.

6 Turn the cooked cake out on to the prepared towel, remove the parchment, and trim the edges. While still warm, roll the cake, then leave to cool slightly.

7 When the cake is almost cool, unroll it, spread with buttercream and roll up again. Dust with icing sugar and cocoa powder, and serve.

Energy 196kcal/826kJ; Protein 2.8g; Carbohydrate 35.1g, of which sugars 29.7g; Fat 5.9g, of which saturates 3g; Cholesterol 73mg; Calcium 34mg; Fibre 0.4g; Sodium 70mg.

BREAD PUDDING

COOKS HAVE ALWAYS BEEN INCREDIBLY INVENTIVE WHEN IT COMES TO USING UP LEFTOVERS.
THIS SPECIAL PUDDING MADE OF STALE BREAD CAN BE SERVED AS A CAKE OR AS A DESSERT WITH
CREAM. IT NEEDS PLENTY OF DRIED FRUIT AND GRATED CITRUS RIND TO SHARPEN THE FLAVOUR.

MAKES 9 SQUARES

INGREDIENTS
    225g/8oz/4 cups stale bread,
      weighed after removing crusts
    300ml/½ pint/1¼ cups milk
    butter, for greasing
    50g/1¾oz/4 tbsp dark muscovado
      (molasses) sugar
    85g/3oz/½ cup shredded suet
      (US chilled, grated shortening) or
      chilled, grated butter
    225g/8oz/1⅓ cups mixed dried fruit,
      including currants, sultanas (golden
      raisins) and chopped citrus peel
    15ml/1 tbsp mixed (apple pie) spice
    2.5ml/½ tsp freshly grated nutmeg
    finely grated rind of 1 small orange
      and 1 small lemon, plus a little
      orange or lemon juice
    1 egg, lightly beaten
    caster (superfine) sugar for sprinkling

1 Break the bread into small pieces. Place the bread in a large mixing bowl, pour the milk over and leave for about 30 minutes.

2 Preheat the oven to 180°C/350°F/ Gas 4. Butter an 18cm/7in square and 5cm/2in deep ovenproof dish. Using a fork, break up the bread in the milk.

3 Stir the sugar, suet, dried fruit, spices and citrus rinds into the bread and milk mixture.

4 Beat in the egg, adding some orange or lemon juice to make a soft mixture.

GRANDMOTHER'S TIP
Although suet is the traditional ingredient in this recipe, you may prefer to use grated chilled butter.

5 Spread the pudding mixture into the prepared dish and level the surface. Put into the hot oven and cook for about 1¼ hours or until the top is brown and firm to the touch.

6 Sprinkle caster sugar over the surface while still warm, then cool slightly before cutting into squares and removing from the dish.

Energy 254kcal/1072kJ; Protein 4.3g; Carbohydrate 39.7g, of which sugars 27g; Fat 10.2g, of which saturates 5.3g; Cholesterol 31mg; Calcium 103mg; Fibre 1.4g; Sodium 147mg.

WALNUT AND DATE CAKE

THIS IS A WONDERFULLY RICH AND MOIST CAKE. IT IS PERFECT FOR AFTERNOON TEA. THE DATES ARE FIRST SOAKED BRIEFLY IN HOT WATER BEFORE ADDING THEM TO THE MIXTURE, WHICH MAKES A SOFT DROPPING BATTER AND GIVES THE CAKE A LOVELY SOFT TEXTURE.

MAKES 18–24 SQUARES

INGREDIENTS
   225g/8oz/1⅓ cups chopped dates
   250ml/8fl oz/1 cup boiling water
   5ml/1 tsp bicarbonate of soda
      (baking soda)
   225g/8oz/generous 1 cup caster
      (superfine) sugar
   1 egg, beaten
   275g/10oz/2¼ cups plain (all-
      purpose) flour
   2.5ml/½ tsp salt
   75g/3oz/6 tbsp butter, softened
   5ml/1 tsp vanilla extract
   5ml/1 tsp baking powder
   50g/2oz/½ cup chopped walnuts

GRANDMOTHER'S TIP
This cake keeps well but if you want it to last a little longer, only cut what you need and store the rest in an airtight container.

1 Put the chopped dates into a warm, dry bowl and pour the boiling water over the top; it should just cover the dates. Add the bicarbonate of soda and mix in thoroughly. Leave to stand for 5–10 minutes.

2 Preheat the oven to 180°C/350°F/ Gas 4. Lightly grease a rectangular 23 x 30cm/9 x 12in cake tin (pan) and line with baking parchment.

3 In a separate mixing bowl, combine all the remaining ingredients for the cake. Then mix in the dates, along with the soaking water until you have a thick batter. You may find it necessary to add a little more boiling water to help the consistency.

4 Pour or spoon the batter into the tin and bake in the oven for 45 minutes. Cut into squares, when cool.

Energy 749kcal/3155kJ; Protein 10.5g; Carbohydrate 125.5g, of which sugars 77.8g; Fat 26.2g, of which saturates 11g; Cholesterol 88mg; Calcium 153mg; Fibre 3.4g; Sodium 141mg.

BANANA BREAD

The important trick in this traditional cake is to use bananas that are really soft and ripe – the blacker the better. It is a thrifty recipe, using up over-ripe bananas that might otherwise have been discarded. Make them into this delicious sweet cake instead.

2 Peel the bananas and slice them into a bowl. Mash them well, then stir them into the cake mixture. Add enough milk to give a dropping consistency.

3 Spoon the mixture into the loaf tin and level the surface. Bake for 1¼ hours or until a skewer inserted in the centre comes out clean. Cool on a wire rack.

MAKES 1 LOAF

INGREDIENTS
    115g/4oz/½ cup butter, plus extra for
      greasing
    5ml/1 tsp bicarbonate of soda
      (baking soda)
    225g/8oz/2 cups wholemeal (whole-
      wheat) flour
    2 eggs, beaten
    3 very ripe bananas
    30–45ml/2–3 tbsp milk

VARIATION
Sunflower seeds make a good addition to banana cake. Add about 50g/2oz/½ cup to the mixture just before baking.

1 Preheat the oven to 180°C/350°F/Gas 4. Grease and base line a 23 x 13cm/ 9 x 5in loaf tin (pan). Cream the butter in a bowl until it is fluffy. Sift the bicarbonate of soda with the flour, then add to the creamed butter, alternately with the eggs.

Per loaf: Energy 1616kcals/5090kJ; Fat, total 66g; saturated fat 17.5g; polyunsaturated fat 15.2g; monounsaturated fat 26.5g; Carbohydrate 215g; sugar, total 70g; starch 145g; Fibre 23.5g; Sodium 2320mg.

MARMALADE TEABREAD

THIS IS A CAKE THAT IS JUST PERFECT FOR SERVING WITH A CUP OF TEA. THE MARMALADE GIVES IT A LOVELY ORANGEY FLAVOUR AND AT THE SAME TIME KEEPS THE MIXTURE MOIST. IF YOU PREFER NOT TO ICE OR DECORATE THIS CAKE IT WOULD BE JUST AS DELICIOUS SERVED SLICED AND BUTTERED.

MAKES 8–10 SLICES

INGREDIENTS
    200g/7oz/1¾ cups plain
      (all-purpose) flour
    5ml/1 tsp baking powder
    6.25ml/1¼ tsp ground cinnamon
    100g/3½oz/7 tbsp butter, cut into
      small pieces
    55g/2oz/3 tbsp soft light
      brown sugar
    1 egg
    60ml/4 tbsp chunky orange
      marmalade
    about 45ml/3 tbsp milk
For the icing
    juice of ½ lemon
    115g/4oz/1 cup icing (confectioners')
      sugar
    shreds of orange and lemon rind,
      to decorate

1 Preheat the oven to 160°C/325°F/ Gas 3. Grease a 450g/1lb loaf tin (pan), and line with baking parchment.

2 Sift the flour, baking powder and cinnamon together, then add the butter and rub in with the fingertips until the mixture resembles fine crumbs. Stir in the sugar.

3 Beat the egg lightly in a small bowl and mix it with the marmalade and most of the milk.

4 Mix the milk mixture into the flour mixture, adding more milk if necessary to give a soft dropping consistency.

5 Transfer the mixture to the prepared tin, put into the hot oven and cook for about 1¼ hours, until the cake is firm to the touch and cooked through.

6 Leave the cake to cool for 5 minutes, then turn on to a wire rack. Peel off the lining paper and leave the cake to cool.

7 Combine the icing sugar and lemon juice to make the icing, and spoon over the top of the cake. Decorate with shreds of orange and lemon rind.

Energy 250kcal/1049kJ; Protein 3.5g; Carbohydrate 38g, of which sugars 19g; Fat 10.4g, of which saturates 6.2g; Cholesterol 48mg; Calcium 56mg; Fibre 0.8g; Sodium 86mg.

CURRANT BREAD

THIS IS A SPECIAL LOAF PACKED TO BURSTING WITH DRIED FRUIT AND SPICES, ALL ROLLED UP IN SWEET YEAST DOUGH. THE FRUIT IS PLUMPED UP BY SIMMERING IT GENTLY IN HOT WATER WHILE THE DOUGH RISES. IT NEEDS NO MORE ADORNMENT THAN BUTTER AND MAYBE A SPOONFUL OF JAM.

MAKES 1 LOAF

INGREDIENTS
 500g/1¼lb/generous 4 cups strong
   white bread flour, plus extra
   for dusting
 2 sachets easy-blend (rapid-rise)
   dried yeast
 250ml/8fl oz/1 cup lukewarm milk
 50g/2oz/¼ cup white caster
   (superfine) sugar
 pinch of ground cinnamon
 pinch of ground nutmeg
 pinch of powdered saffron
 1 egg yolk, lightly beaten
 50g/2oz/¼ cup butter, softened, plus
   extra for greasing
 10ml/2 tsp salt
For the filling
 150g/5oz/⅔ cup currants
 150g/5oz/1 cup raisins
 50g/2oz/⅓ cup finely diced
   glacé (candied) citron peel
 50g/2oz/⅓ cup glacé (candied)
   orange peel

GRANDMOTHER'S TIP
Before rolling up the dough at the end of step 6, shape 200g/7oz almond paste into a roll, place on the dough rectangle, roll up and continue as above.

1 Sift the flour into a bowl and make a well in the centre. Add the yeast and a little of the milk to the well and mix together, incorporating some of the flour. Add 5ml/1 tsp of the sugar, cover the bowl with a clean dish towel and leave to stand for 10 minutes.

2 Add the cinnamon, nutmeg and saffron to the remaining milk, add to the bowl and mix well. Add the egg yolk, the remaining sugar and the butter and knead briefly, then add the salt.

3 Turn out the dough on to a lightly floured surface and knead vigorously for at least 15 minutes, until the dough is no longer sticky and is full of bubbles, add a little extra milk if necessary.

4 Shape the dough into a ball, return to a clean bowl and cover with a dampened dish towel. Leave at room temperature for 1 hour, until it has doubled in bulk.

5 To make the filling, poach the currants with the raisins in plenty of simmering water for 10 minutes. Drain well and pat dry in a cloth.

6 Turn out the dough and knead in the dried fruit and both types of glacé fruit peel. Dust both the dough and the work surface with flour and roll into a rectangle 30cm/12in wide. Brush the flour away on both sides. Roll up the rectangle, starting at the top or bottom, wherever the filling is most sparse.

7 Grease a 30 x 10 x 10-cm/12 x 10 x 10-in loaf tin (pan) with butter. Place the dough roll in the tin, with the final fold underneath. Cover with a damp dish towel and leave at room temperature for about 1 hour, until the dough has just risen above the rim. Preheat the oven to 200°C/400°F/Gas 6.

8 Bake the loaf for 35 minutes, then brush the top with cold water and return to the oven for 1 minute. Turn out on to a wire rack and leave to cool.

Per loaf: Energy 3375kcal/14303kJ; Protein 57.3g; Carbohydrate 705.8g, of which sugars 324.8g; Fat 55.2g, of which saturates 28.6g; Cholesterol 308mg; Calcium 1098mg; Fibre 26.2g; Sodium 4651mg.

COTTAGE LOAF

NOTHING COULD BE MORE TRADITIONAL THAN A PLUMP, ROUND COTTAGE LOAF. THIS CLASSIC SHAPE WITH ITS SMALL LOAF SITTING ON TOP OF THE BIGGER BASE IS BOUND TO APPEAL TO CHILDREN. THE OLD TRICK OF SNIPPING THE DOUGH ROUND THE EDGES GIVES IT ROOM TO EXPAND IN THE OVEN.

MAKES 1 LARGE ROUND LOAF

INGREDIENTS
  675g/1½lb/6 cups unbleached strong white bread flour
  10ml/2 tsp salt
  20g/¾ oz fresh yeast
  400ml/14fl oz/1⅔ cups lukewarm water

1 Lightly grease 2 baking sheets. Sift the flour and salt together into a large bowl and make a well in the centre.

2 Mix the yeast in 150ml/¼ pint/⅔ cup of the water until dissolved. Pour into the centre of the flour with the remaining water and mix to a firm dough.

3 Knead on a lightly floured surface for 10 minutes until smooth and elastic. Place in a lightly oiled bowl, cover with lightly oiled clear film (plastic wrap) and leave to rise, in a warm place, for about 1 hour, or until doubled in bulk.

4 Turn out on to a lightly floured surface and knock back (punch down). Knead for 2–3 minutes, then divide the dough into two-thirds and one-third; shape into balls.

5 Place the balls of dough on the prepared baking sheets. Cover with inverted bowls and leave to rise, in a warm place, for about 30 minutes (see Grandmother's Tips).

6 Gently flatten the top of the larger round of dough and, with a sharp knife, cut a cross in the centre, about 4cm/1½in wide. Brush with a little water and place the smaller round on top.

7 Carefully press a hole through the middle of the top ball, down into the lower part, using your thumb and first two fingers of one hand.

8 Cover the loaf with lightly oiled clear film and leave to rest in a warm place for about 10 minutes.

9 After the dough has rested, turn the oven on to 220°C/425°F/Gas 7 and place the bread on the lower shelf. The loaf will finish expanding as the oven heats up.

10 Bake for 35–40 minutes, or until the loaf is golden brown and sounding hollow when tapped. Cool on a wire rack.

GRANDMOTHER'S TIPS
• To ensure a good-shaped cottage loaf the dough needs to be firm enough to support the weight of the top ball.
• Do not over-prove the dough on the second rising or the loaf may topple over – but it will still taste good.

Per loaf: Energy 2302Kcal/9788kJ; Protein 63.5g; Carbohydrate 524.5g, of which sugars 10.1g; Fat 8.8g, of which saturates 1.4g; Cholesterol 0mg; Calcium 946mg; Fibre 20.9g; Sodium 3950mg.

FARMHOUSE LOAF

IN BAKERIES THIS HOMELY LOAF IS CALLED A SPLIT TIN LOAF BECAUSE OF THE WAY THE CRUST IS SPLIT DOWN THE MIDDLE. YOU COULD TRY MAKING IT AS TRADITIONAL BAKERS USED TO DO, WITH TWO SEPARATE PIECES OF DOUGH IN ONE TIN, WHICH JOIN UP AND LEAVE A CRACK WHEN BAKED.

MAKES 1 LOAF

INGREDIENTS
 500g/1¼ lb/5 cups strong white
   bread flour, plus extra for dusting
 10ml/2 tsp salt
 15g/½ oz fresh yeast
 300ml/½ pint/1¼ cups lukewarm
   water
 60ml/4 tbsp lukewarm milk

1 Lightly grease a 900g/2lb loaf tin (pan) 18.5 x 11.5cm/7¼ x 4½in. Sift the flour and salt together into a large bowl and make a well in the centre. Mix the yeast with half the lukewarm water in a bowl, then stir in the remaining water.

2 Pour the yeast mixture into the centre of the flour, and using your fingers, mix in a little flour. Gradually mix in a little more of the flour from around the edge of the bowl to form a thick, smooth batter.

3 Sprinkle a little more flour from around the edge over the top of the batter, and then leave in a warm place to 'sponge'.

4 After about 20 minutes, bubbles will appear in the batter. At this stage, pour in the milk and then gradually combine the remaining flour into the batter, and mix to a firm dough.

5 Place on a floured surface and knead for about 10 minutes until smooth and elastic. Place in a lightly oiled bowl, cover with lightly oiled clear film (plastic wrap) and leave to rise, in a warm place, for 1–1¼ hours, until doubled in size.

6 Knock back (punch down) the dough and turn out on to a floured surface. Shape into a rectangle, the length of the tin. Roll up lengthways, tuck the ends under and place seam side down in the tin. Cover and leave in a warm place for about 20 minutes.

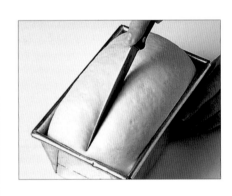

7 Using a sharp knife, make a deep slash down the length of the bread; dust with flour. Leave for 10–15 minutes.

8 Meanwhile, preheat the oven to 230°C/450°F/Gas 8. Bake for 15 minutes, then reduce the oven temperature to 200°C/400°F/Gas 6. Bake for 20–25 minutes more, or until the bread is golden and sounds hollow when tapped on the base. Turn out on to a wire rack to cool.

Per loaf: Energy 1733kcal/7367kJ; Protein 49g; Carbohydrate 391.5g, of which sugars 10.5g; Fat 7.5g, of which saturates 1.6g; Cholesterol 4mg; Calcium 773mg; Fibre 15.5g; Sodium 3978mg.

BROWN SODA BREAD

THIS IRISH SPECIALITY IS BEST EATEN ON THE DAY OF BAKING SO THAT EVERYONE APPRECIATES ITS LOVELY RUSTIC FLAVOUR. IT IS ESPECIALLY GOOD WITH FRESH BUTTER, STRONG FARMHOUSE CHEESE AND SOME CRISP STICKS OF CELERY OR A BOWL OF HOME-MADE SOUP.

MAKES 1 LOAF

INGREDIENTS
    450g/1lb/4 cups wholemeal (whole-wheat) flour, plus extra for dusting
    175g/6oz/1½ cups plain (all-purpose) flour
    7.5ml/1½ tsp bicarbonate of soda (baking soda)
    5ml/1 tsp salt
    about 450ml/¾ pint/scant 2 cups buttermilk

GRANDMOTHER'S TIP
If you can't find buttermilk for this recipe, you can try mixing plain yogurt or lemon juice to fresh milk, this works in a similar way to buttermilk. Another way to provide the acid is to add 7.5ml/1½ tsp cream of tartar to the dry ingredients.

1 Preheat the oven to 200°C/400°F/Gas 6, and grease a baking sheet. Combine the dry ingredients in a mixing bowl and stir in enough buttermilk to make a fairly soft dough. Turn on to a work surface dusted with wholemeal flour and knead lightly until smooth. Form the dough into a circle, about 4cm/1½in thick.

2 Place on the baking sheet and mark a deep cross in the top with a knife.

3 Bake for about 45 minutes, or until the bread is browned and sounds hollow when tapped on the base. Cool on a wire rack. If a soft crust is preferred, wrap the loaf in a clean dish towel while cooling.

Per loaf: Energy 2262Kcal/9643kJ; Protein 88.5g; Carbohydrate 465.4g, of which sugars 31.4g; Fat 18.9g, of which saturates 6.5g; Cholesterol 27mg; Calcium 1.37g; Fibre 34.2g; Sodium 2.18g.

DROP SCONES

These little scones are known by many different names, such as griddle cakes or Scotch pancakes. They make a quick and easy warm breakfast, or a special treat for elevenses or at tea time, topped with butter and jam or drizzled with honey.

2 Add the diced butter and rub it into the flour with your fingertips until the mixture resembles fine, evenly textured breadcrumbs.

3 Make a well in the centre of the flour mixture, then stir in the egg.

4 Add the milk a little at a time, stirring it in to check consistency. Add enough milk to give a lovely thick, creamy consistency.

5 Cook in batches. Drop 3 or 4 evenly sized spoonfuls of the mixture, spaced slightly apart, on the griddle or frying pan. Cook over a medium heat for 2–3 minutes, until bubbles rise to the surface and burst.

6 Turn the scones over and cook for a further 2–3 minutes, until golden underneath. Place the cooked scones between the folds of a clean dish towel while cooking the remaining batter. Serve warm, with butter and honey.

MAKES 8-10

INGREDIENTS
  115g/4oz/1 cup plain
    (all-purpose) flour
  5ml/1 tsp bicarbonate of soda
    (baking soda)
  5ml/1 tsp cream of tartar
  25g/1oz/2 tbsp butter, diced
  1 egg, beaten
  about 150ml/¼ pint/⅔ cup milk
  butter and honey, to serve

GRANDMOTHER'S TIP
Placing the cooked scones in a clean, folded dish towel keeps them soft and moist. Bring to the table like this and ask your guests to pull them out and serve themselves.

1 Lightly grease a griddle pan or heavy frying pan, then preheat it. Sift the flour, bicarbonate of soda and cream of tartar together into a mixing bowl.

Energy 90kcal/379kJ; Protein 2.8g; Carbohydrate 12.1g, of which sugars 1.1g; Fat 3.8g, of which saturates 2.1g; Cholesterol 32mg; Calcium 47mg; Fibre 0.5g; Sodium 36mg.

CRUMPETS

TOASTED CRUMPETS ARE A TREAT FOR ALL AGES, BUT ARE PARTICULARLY ASSOCIATED WITH NURSERY TEAS IN VICTORIAN TIMES, WHEN THEY WOULD HAVE BEEN BROWNED ON A FORK BY THE FIRE. THE YEAST BATTER IS FIRST COOKED IN METAL RINGS ON A GRIDDLE AND LEFT TO COOL BEFORE TOASTING.

MAKES ABOUT 10

INGREDIENTS
- 225g/8oz/2 cups plain (all-purpose) flour
- 2.5ml/½ tsp salt
- 2.5ml/½ tsp bicarbonate of soda (baking soda)
- 5ml/1 tsp easy-blend (rapid-rise) dried yeast
- 150ml/¼ pint/⅔ cup milk
- oil, for greasing

1 Sift the flour, salt and bicarbonate of soda into a bowl and stir in the yeast. Make a well in the centre. Heat the milk with 200ml/7fl oz/scant 1 cup water until lukewarm, and pour slowly into the well.

2 Mix well with a whisk or wooden spoon, beating vigorously to make a thick, smooth batter. Cover and leave in a warm place for about 1 hour until the mixture has a spongy texture.

3 Heat a griddle or heavy frying pan. Lightly oil the hot surface and the inside of three or four metal rings, each measuring about 8cm/3½in in diameter. Place the oiled rings on the hot surface and leave for 1–2 minutes until hot.

4 Spoon the batter into the rings to a depth of about 1cm/½in. Cook over a medium-high heat for about 6 minutes, until the top surface is set and bubbles have burst open to make holes.

5 When set, carefully lift off the metal rings and flip the crumpets over, cooking the second side for just 1 minute until lightly browned.

6 Remove from the pan and leave to cool completely on a wire rack. Repeat with the remaining crumpet mixture.

7 Just before serving, toast the crumpets under a grill (broiler) on both sides, and butter generously.

Energy 93kcal/393kJ; Protein 3g; Carbohydrate 16.5g, of which sugars 1g; Fat 2.1g, of which saturates 1g; Cholesterol 21mg; Calcium 48mg; Fibre 0.6g; Sodium 21mg.

BAKES AND COOKIES

*In this chapter you will find recipes for all
kinds of individual small cakes, cookies and tray
bakes that probably sum up the best of home
baking. These delicious morsels make the most of
store-cupboard ingredients and are ideal
for filling the hunger gap between meals,
serving with afternoon tea or for packing into
a lunch box for a special treat.*

GINGERBREAD

MAKING GINGERBREAD BRINGS BACK THE SCENTS AND TASTES OF CHILDHOOD TO THE KITCHEN, WITH THE AROMA OF WARM HONEY AND GINGER FILLING THE AIR. THIS VERSION ADDS CHOPPED TOASTED HAZELNUTS FOR A RUSTIC CRUNCH. IT IS VERY EASY TO MAKE AND WILL PROVE A REAL WINNER.

MAKES 30 SQUARES

INGREDIENTS
   300g/11oz/scant 3 cups hazelnuts
   300g/11oz/1½ cups soft dark
     brown sugar
   5 eggs
   150g/5oz/10 tbsp butter
   100g/3½oz/½ cup honey
   500g/1⅛lb/5 cups plain (all-purpose)
     flour
   25ml/5 tsp baking powder
   7.5ml/1½ tsp ground ginger

1 Preheat the oven to 160°C/325°F/ Gas 3 and line a 40 x 30cm/16 x 12in baking tray with baking parchment.

2 Toast the hazelnuts in a frying pan over medium heat, moving them around so they brown evenly. Cool, then chop.

3 Melt the butter in a small pan. Beat the sugar with the eggs until the mixture is light and thick.

4 Stir the melted butter, honey and hazelnuts into the egg mixture. Sift the flour with the baking powder and ground ginger and fold into the mixture. Pour the batter into the prepared tray. Bake for about 45 minutes. Cool in the tin before cutting into squares.

Energy 741kcal/3106kJ; Protein 14.1g; Carbohydrate 89.1g, of which sugars 45.4g; Fat 38.9g, of which saturates 11.5g; Cholesterol 144mg; Calcium 166mg; Fibre 3.8g; Sodium 171mg.

YORKSHIRE PARKIN

THIS MOIST GINGER CAKE IS TRADITIONALLY SERVED CUT INTO SQUARES, AS A FILLING TEATIME TREAT OR A DESSERT WITH APPLE SAUCE. IT IS BASED ON A NOURISHING OATMEAL AND FLOUR MIXTURE, WITH PLENTY OF DARK AND LIGHT SYRUP TO SWEETEN THE CAKE AND BLEND WITH THE GINGER.

MAKES 16–20 SQUARES

INGREDIENTS
    300ml/½ pint/1¼ cups milk
    225g/8oz/1 cup golden (corn) syrup
    225g/8oz/¾ cup treacle (molasses)
    115g/4oz/½ cup butter
    50g/2oz/scant ¼ cup soft dark
      brown sugar
    450g/1lb/4 cups plain (all-purpose)
      flour
    2.5ml/½ tsp bicarbonate of soda
      (baking soda)
    7.5ml/1½ tsp ground ginger
    350g/12oz/4 cups medium oatmeal
    1 egg, beaten
    icing (confectioner's) sugar, to dust

1 Preheat the oven to 180°C/350°F/ Gas 4. Grease a 20cm/8in square cake tin (pan) and line the base and sides with baking parchment.

2 Gently heat together the milk, syrup, treacle, butter and sugar, stirring until smooth; do not boil.

3 Sift the flour into a bowl, and add the bicarbonate of soda, ginger and oatmeal. Make a well in the centre of the dry ingredients and add the egg.

4 Stir the egg into the flour and then add the warmed milk and treacle mixture, stirring well until you have a smooth batter.

5 Pour the batter into the tin and bake in the oven for about 45 minutes, until the top is firm to the touch. Cool slightly in the tin, then turn out onto a wire rack to cool completely. Cut into squares and dust with icing sugar.

Energy 273kcal/1152kJ; Protein 5.3g; Carbohydrate 50g, of which sugars 20.1g; Fat 7.1g, of which saturates 3.3g; Cholesterol 23mg; Calcium 127mg; Fibre 1.9g; Sodium 102mg.

COCONUT MACAROONS

THESE DELICATE, AROMATIC CAKES ARE SIMPLE FOR CHILDREN TO MAKE WITH A LITTLE SUPERVISION, AS JUST A FEW INGREDIENTS ARE NEEDED. THEY ARE BEST SERVED WARM, STRAIGHT FROM THE OVEN, BUT WILL KEEP REASONABLY WELL IN AN AIRTIGHT CONTAINER.

MAKES 15–20

INGREDIENTS
    1 vanilla pod (bean)
    120ml/4fl oz/½ cup double
       (heavy) cream
    200g/7oz desiccated (dry
       unsweetened shredded) coconut
    200g/4oz/1 cup caster (superfine)
       sugar
    1 egg

1 Put the vanilla pod in a pan with the cream. Bring to a simmer then turn off the heat and infuse for 20 minutes.

2 Preheat the oven to 200°C/400°F/ Gas 6. Line a baking sheet. Remove the pod from the cream and pour the cream into a large bowl. Mix in the coconut, sugar and egg.

3 Spoon the mixture in piles on to the prepared baking sheet. Bake for 12–15 minutes until golden brown. Leave the cakes to cool slightly before transferring to a cooling rack.

Energy 177kcal/740kJ; Protein 1.4g; Carbohydrate 14.9g, of which sugars 14.9g; Fat 13g, of which saturates 9.9g; Cholesterol 23.6mg; Calcium 16mg; Fibre 1.8g; Sodium 10.9mg.

HONEY <u>AND</u> SPICE CAKES

THESE GOLDEN CAKES FROM WALES ARE FRAGRANT WITH HONEY AND CINNAMON. THEY RISE QUITE SPECTACULARLY IN THE OVEN, SO LEAVE PLENTY OF ROOM IN EACH CAKE CASE. ONE OF THESE WOULD BE AN IDEAL ADDITION TO A CHILD'S LUNCH BOX OR AS A SWEET TREAT FOR ELEVENSES.

MAKES 18

INGREDIENTS
    250g/9oz/2 cups plain (all-purpose)
      flour
    5ml/1 tsp ground cinnamon
    5ml/1 tsp bicarbonate of soda
      (baking soda)
    125g/4½oz/½ cup butter, softened
    125g/4½oz/10 tbsp soft light
      brown sugar
    1 large (US extra large) egg,
      separated
    125g/4½oz clear honey
    about 60ml/4 tbsp milk
    caster (superfine) sugar for sprinkling

1 Preheat the oven to 200°C/400°F/
Gas 6. Butter the holes of a muffin tin
(pan) or line them with paper cases.

2 Sift the flour, cinnamon and
bicarbonate of soda into a large bowl.

3 Beat the butter with the sugar until
light and fluffy. Beat in the egg yolk,
then gradually add the honey.

4 With a large metal spoon and a
cutting action, fold in the flour mixture
plus sufficient milk to make a soft
mixture that will just drop off the spoon.

5 In a separate bowl whisk the egg
white until stiff peaks form. Using a
large metal spoon, fold the egg white
into the cake mixture.

6 Divide the mixture among the paper
cases or the holes in the prepared tin.
Put into the hot oven and cook for
15–20 minutes or until risen, firm to
the touch and golden brown.

7 Sprinkle the tops lightly with caster
sugar and leave to cool completely on
a wire rack.

Energy 152kcal/639kJ; Protein 1.9g; Carbohydrate 23.6g, of which sugars 13g; Fat 6.3g, of which saturates 3.8g; Cholesterol 26mg; Calcium 30mg; Fibre 0.4g; Sodium 49mg.

RASPBERRY CRUMBLE BUNS

THESE FRUITY LITTLE CAKES ARE BEST MADE IN HIGH SUMMER, WHEN RASPBERRIES ARE BURSTING WITH FLAVOUR. THE NUTTY CRUMBLE TOPPING CONTRASTS BEAUTIFULLY WITH THE SOFT FRUIT INSIDE. THESE CAKES CAN BE SERVED WITH RASPBERRY JAM AND CREAM FOR A SPECIAL TREAT.

MAKES 12

INGREDIENTS
    175g/6oz/1½ cups plain (all-purpose)
      flour
    10ml/2 tsp baking powder
    5ml/1 tsp ground cinnamon
    115g/4oz/½ cup butter, melted
    120ml/4fl oz/½ cup milk
    50g/2oz/¼ cup caster (superfine)
      sugar
    50g/2oz/¼ cup soft light brown sugar
    1 egg
    225g/8oz/1⅓ cups fresh raspberries
    grated rind of 1 lemon
For the crumble topping
    50g/2oz/½ cup pecan nuts, finely
      chopped
    50g/2oz/¼ cup soft dark brown sugar
    45ml/3 tbsp plain (all-purpose) flour
    5ml/1 tsp ground cinnamon
    40g/1½oz/3 tbsp butter, melted

1 Preheat the oven to 180°C/350°F/ Gas 4. Arrange 12 paper cases in a muffin tin (pan).

2 Sift the flour, baking powder and cinnamon into a large bowl. In another bowl, beat together the cooled, melted butter and milk.

3 Make a well in the centre of the flour and add the two types of sugar, then the egg. Add the melted butter and milk mixture and stir in gradually until just combined. Don't overmix, as this will make the buns heavier when cooked.

4 Stir the raspberries and lemon rind into the mixture, then spoon into the muffin cases, filling almost to the top.

5 To make the crumble topping, mix the chopped pecans, sugar, flour and cinnamon in a large mixing bowl. Stir in the melted butter to coat everything and create a crumbly texture.

6 Spoon a little of the crumble over the top of each bun. Bake for about 25 minutes until they are risen and golden.

7 Leave to stand for 5 minutes, then transfer to a wire rack to cool slightly. Serve while still warm.

Energy 251kcal/1051kJ; Protein 3.4g; Carbohydrate 28.9g, of which sugars 14.9g; Fat 14.4g, of which saturates 7.5g; Cholesterol 46mg; Calcium 56mg; Fibre 1.2g; Sodium 110mg.

MAIDS OF HONOUR

THESE LITTLE DELICACIES ARE SAID TO DATE FROM THE REIGN OF HENRY VIII. IN PAST TIMES THEY WOULD HAVE BEEN FILLED WITH STRAINED CURDS, BUT THESE DAYS THEY ARE MADE WITH A SHARP CURD CHEESE FILLING, WELL FLAVOURED WITH GROUND ALMONDS, LEMON AND SUGAR.

MAKES 12

INGREDIENTS
250g/9oz ready-made puff pastry
250g/9oz/1¼ cups curd (farmer's)
  cheese
60ml/4 tbsp ground almonds
45ml/3 tbsp caster (superfine) sugar
finely grated rind of 1 small lemon
2 eggs
15g/½ oz/1 tbsp butter, melted
icing (confectioner's) sugar, to dust

1 Preheat the oven to 200°C/400°F/ Gas 6. Butter a muffin tin (pan).

2 Roll out the puff pastry very thinly on a lightly floured surface and, using a 7.5/3in cutter, cut out 12 circles. Press the pastry circles into the prepared tray and prick well with a fork. Chill, while you make the filling.

3 Put the curd cheese into a bowl and add the almonds, sugar and lemon rind. Lightly beat the eggs with the butter and add to the cheese mixture. Mix well.

4 Spoon the mixture into the pastry cases. Bake for about 20 minutes, until the pastry is well risen and the filling is puffed up, golden brown and just firm to the touch.

5 Transfer to a wire rack (the filling will sink down as it cools). Serve warm or at room temperature, dusted with a little sifted icing sugar.

Energy 182kcal/758kJ; Protein 5.2g; Carbohydrate 12.6g, of which sugars 5.1g; Fat 12.9g, of which saturates 3g; Cholesterol 43mg; Calcium 31mg; Fibre 0.4g; Sodium 85mg.

CUSTARD TARTS

THESE TARTS ARE AN INDULGENT TREAT, REDOLENT OF TEAS BY THE FIRE IN WINTER OR PICNICS ON THE LAWN IN SUMMER. THE SWEET PASTRY CONTAINS A DELICATELY FLAVOURED EGG CUSTARD, WITH NUTMEG LIBERALLY SPRINKLED ON TOP. USE UP THE LEFTOVER EGG WHITES TO MAKE MERINGUES.

MAKES ABOUT 8

INGREDIENTS
    175g/6oz/1½ cups plain
        (all-purpose) flour
    pinch of salt
    75g/3oz/6 tbsp unsalted butter, at
        room temperature
    75g/3oz/6 tbsp caster (superfine)
        sugar
    3 egg yolks, at room temperature
    a few drops vanilla extract
For the filling
    600ml/1 pint/2½ cups full cream
        (whole) milk
    6 egg yolks
    75g/3oz/6 tbsp caster (superfine)
        sugar
    freshly grated nutmeg

1 To make the pastry, sift the flour and salt into a bowl.

2 Put the butter, sugar, egg yolks and vanilla extract in a food processor and process until the mixture resembles scrambled eggs. Add the flour and blend briefly.

3 Transfer the dough to a lightly floured surface and knead gently until smooth. Form into a ball, flatten and wrap in clear film (plastic wrap). Chill for at least 30 minutes. Bring back to room temperature before rolling out.

4 Roll out the pastry and line eight individual 10cm/4in loose-bottomed tartlet tins (pans). Chill for 30 minutes.

5 Preheat the oven to 200°C/400°F/Gas 6. To make the custard filling, gently heat the milk in a pan until just warmed but not yet boiling.

6 In a bowl, vigorously beat the egg yolks and sugar together until they become pale and creamy in texture.

7 Pour the milk on to the egg mixture and stir well with a wooden spoon to mix. Do not whisk as this will produce too many bubbles.

8 Strain the milk mixture into a jug (pitcher), then carefully pour the liquid into the tartlet cases. Grate fresh nutmeg over the surface of the tartlets.

9 Bake for about 10 minutes, then lower the heat to 180°C/350°F/Gas 4 and bake for another 10 minutes, or until the filling has set and is just turning golden. The tartlets should be a bit wobbly when they come out of the oven. Remove from the oven and lift the tarts out of the tins. Serve warm or cold.

Energy 336kcal/1409kJ; Protein 7.9g; Carbohydrate 40g, of which sugars 23.4g; Fat 17.1g, of which saturates 8.6g; Cholesterol 257mg; Calcium 157mg; Fibre 0.7g; Sodium 101mg.

ALMOND SHORTBREAD

THIS CLASSIC SCOTTISH RECIPE CAN BE MADE VERY QUICKLY AND EASILY IN A FOOD PROCESSOR, OR BY HAND IN THE TRADITIONAL WAY, WHICH TAKES SLIGHTLY LONGER. THE GROUND ALMONDS ADD TASTE AND CRUNCH AND THE RESULTING BUTTERY, CRUMBLY BISCUITS ARE DELIGHTFUL.

MAKES ABOUT 18 FINGERS

INGREDIENTS
    oil, for greasing
    275g/10oz/2½ cups plain
      (all-purpose) flour
    25g/1oz/¼ cup ground almonds
    225g/8oz/1 cup butter, softened
    75g/3oz/scant ½ cup caster
      (superfine) sugar
    grated rind of ½ lemon

VARIATION
You can replace the lemon rind with the grated rind of two oranges for a tangy orange flavour, if you prefer.

1 Preheat the oven to 180°C/350°F/ Gas 4 and oil a 28 x 18cm/11 x 7in shallow cake tin (pan).

2 Put all the ingredients into a blender or food processor and pulse until the mixture comes together.

3 Place the mixture on the oiled tray and flatten it out with a palette knife or metal spatula until evenly spread. Bake in the preheated oven for 20 minutes, or until pale golden brown.

4 Remove from the oven and immediately mark the shortbread into fingers or squares while the mixture is soft. Allow to cool a little, and then transfer to a wire rack and leave until cold. The shortbread should keep for up to two weeks in an airtight container.

GRANDMOTHER'S TIP
To make the shortbread by hand instead of using a food processor, sift the flour and almonds on to a pastry board or work surface. Cream together the butter and sugar in a mixing bowl and then turn the creamed mixture out on to the pastry board with the flour and almonds. Work the mixture together using your fingertips. It should come together to make a smooth dough. Continue to follow the recipe from Step 3.

Energy 64kcal/266kJ; Protein 0.7g; Carbohydrate 6.1g, of which sugars 1.8g; Fat 4.2g, of which saturates 2.5g; Cholesterol 10mg; Calcium 11mg; Fibre 0.2g; Sodium 29mg.

GINGER BISCUITS

THIS RECIPE PRODUCES SPICY BISCUITS THAT MAKE THE MOST OF SEVERAL DIFFERENT FLAVOURINGS. A COMBINATION OF TRADITIONAL STORE-CUPBOARD SPICES — GINGER, CINNAMON AND CLOVES, WITH THE SURPRISE OF A LITTLE CARDAMOM AND BLACK PEPPER — GIVES THEM AN UNUSUAL TWIST.

MAKES 24–28

INGREDIENTS
    100ml/3½fl oz/scant ½ cup golden
      (light corn) syrup
    5ml/1 tsp grated orange rind
    5ml/1 tsp ground cinnamon
    2.5ml/½ tsp ground pepper
    2.5ml/½ tsp ground ginger
    2.5ml/½ tsp ground cloves
    5ml/1 tsp ground cardamom
    10ml/2 tsp bicarbonate of soda
      (baking soda)
    100ml/3½fl oz/scant ½ cup double
      (heavy) cream
    200g/7oz/scant 1 cup unsalted
      butter, softened
    100g/3¾oz/generous ½ cup caster
      (superfine) sugar
    1 egg, beaten
    400g/14oz/3½ cups plain
      (all-purpose) flour

GRANDMOTHER'S TIP
When spooning syrup from the tin, use a metal spoon, dipped in just boiled water. The hot metal will mean the syrup slips off it straight away. If possible, weigh it in the pan in which you intend to heat it.

1 Put the golden syrup, orange rind, cinnamon, pepper, ginger, cloves and cardamom in a pan and heat gently until warm. Remove from the heat.

2 Mix the bicarbonate of soda into the cream so that it is evenly distributed. Put the butter and sugar in a large bowl and whisk together until light and fluffy. Keep whisking as you add the beaten egg, and then the warm spiced syrup. Mix together well.

3 Add the flour to the bowl and mix together to form a dough. Wrap in clear film (plastic wrap) and leave to rest in the refrigerator for at least 1 hour.

4 Preheat the oven to 200°C/400°F/ Gas 6. On a lightly floured surface, roll out the dough to a 3mm/⅛in thickness.

5 Using a cookie cutter or shapes, cut out the dough, re-rolling and cutting out the dough trimmings.

6 Place on a baking sheet and bake in the oven for 7–10 minutes, until light brown. Remove from the sheet and leave to cool on a wire tray.

Energy 1039kcal/4349kJ; Protein 12.4g; Carbohydrate 125.6g, of which sugars 48.1g; Fat 57.7g, of which saturates 35.1g; Cholesterol 188mg; Calcium 193mg; Fibre 3.1g; Sodium 399mg.

MELTING MOMENTS

AS THE NAME SUGGESTS, THESE CRISP BISCUITS REALLY DO MELT IN THE MOUTH. THEY HAVE A SHORTBREAD TEXTURE AND ARE ROLLED IN OATS FOR EXTRA CRUNCH. THEY ARE TRADITIONALLY TOPPED WITH A LITTLE PIECE OF GLACE CHERRY, WHICH MAKES THEM LOOK MOST ATTRACTIVE.

MAKES 16–20

INGREDIENTS
40g/1½oz/3 tbsp soft butter
65g/2½oz/5 tbsp lard or white
  cooking fat
85g/3oz/6 tbsp caster (superfine)
  sugar
1 egg yolk, beaten
few drops of vanilla extract
150g/5oz/1¼ cups self-raising (self-
  rising) flour
rolled oats, for coating
4–5 glacé (candied) cherries

VARIATION
If you wish, use almond extract instead of the vanilla extract, and place an almond on top in place of the cherry.

1 Preheat the oven to 180°C/350°F/ Gas 4. Beat together the butter, lard and sugar, then gradually beat in the egg yolk and vanilla extract.

2 Sift the flour over, and stir to make a soft dough. Roll into 16–20 small balls.

3 Spread rolled oats on a sheet of baking parchment and toss the balls in them until evenly coated.

4 Place the balls, spaced slightly apart so they have room to spread, on two baking sheets. Flatten each ball a little with your thumb.

5 Cut the cherries into quarters and place a quarter of cherry on top of each biscuit (cookie). Put the baking sheets into the hot oven and cook for 15–20 minutes, until they are lightly browned.

6 Allow the biscuits to cool for a few minutes on the baking sheets before transferring them to a wire rack to cool completely.

Energy 88kcal/370kJ; Protein 0.7g; Carbohydrate 10.9g, of which sugars 5.4g; Fat 5g, of which saturates 2.4g; Cholesterol 7mg; Calcium 30mg; Fibre 0.3g; Sodium 40mg.

ALMOND BISCUITS

THESE INTRIGUING ALMOND SHAPES ARE MADE WITH A SMOOTH DOUGH, WHICH IS ROLLED OUT THINLY AND SHAPED INTO A TWIST. CHILDREN WILL REALLY ENJOY THE ROLLING AND SHAPING PROCESS. THEY CAN BE SERVED WITH COFFEE OR ALONGSIDE A CREAMY FOOL OR ICE-CREAM DESSERT.

MAKES 20

INGREDIENTS
    200g/7oz/1 cup sugar
    150g/5oz/10 tbsp butter
    3 eggs
    350g/12oz/3 cups plain
      (all-purpose) flour, plus extra for
      dusting
    100g/3¾oz/scant 1 cup ground
      almonds
    caster (superfine) sugar, and chopped
      almonds, to decorate

GRANDMOTHER'S TIP
If you are making these with children, try shaping the biscuits into letters.

1 Preheat the oven to 180°C/350°F/ Gas 4. Put the sugar and butter in a large bowl and beat until light and fluffy. Add the eggs, one at a time, beating after each addition.

2 When all the eggs are incorporated, add the flour and almonds to the bowl and mix thoroughly to make a dough.

3 On a floured surface, roll out the dough quite thinly and cut into strips. Cut the strips into 4cm/1½in lengths.

4 Twist each strip into an S shape. Place on a baking tray. Sprinkle with sugar and chopped almonds. Bake for 10 minutes, until golden brown.

Energy 188kcal/788kJ; Protein 3.5g; Carbohydrate 22.5g, of which sugars 10.9g; Fat 10g, of which saturates 4.4g; Cholesterol 45mg; Calcium 44mg; Fibre 0.8g; Sodium 58mg.

BUTTER COOKIES

THESE CRUNCHY, BUTTERY COOKIES MAKE A DELICIOUS AFTER-SCHOOL TREAT SERVED WITH A GLASS OF MILK. THE CLEVER FEATURE OF THESE SWEET COOKIES IS THAT THE DOUGH CAN BE MADE WELL IN ADVANCE AND CHILLED UNTIL YOU ARE READY TO SLICE IT AND BAKE A FRESH BATCH.

MAKES 25–30

INGREDIENTS
175g/6oz/¾ cup unsalted butter, at room temperature, diced
90g/3½oz/½ cup golden caster (superfine) sugar
250g/9oz/2¼ cups plain (all-purpose) flour
demerara (raw) sugar, for coating

VARIATIONS
• To flavour the cookies, add ground cinnamon, grated lemon or orange rind, or vanilla or almond extract to the butter mixture. You can also try adding whole glacé (candied) cherries, or chocolate chips, chopped nuts or dried fruit such as chopped apricots to the dough when you add the flour.
• As an alternative, coat the outside in a mixture of sugar and chopped nuts.

1 Put the butter and sugar in a bowl and beat until light and fluffy. Add the flour and, using your hands, gradually work it in until the mixture forms a smooth dough.

2 Roll the dough into a sausage shape about 30cm/12in long, then pat to form either a square or triangular log.

3 Sprinkle a thick layer of demerara sugar on a piece of baking parchment paper. Press each side of the dough into the sugar to coat. Wrap and chill for about 30 minutes until firm. Meanwhile, preheat the oven to 160°C/325°F/Gas 3.

4 When ready to bake, remove the dough from the refrigerator and unwrap it. Cut into thick slices and place slightly apart on non-stick baking sheets. Bake for 20 minutes until just beginning to turn brown. Transfer to a wire rack to cool.

Energy 84Kcal/350kJ; Protein 0.8g; Carbohydrate 9.6g, of which sugars 3.3g; Fat 4.9g, of which saturates 3.1g; Cholesterol 12mg; Calcium 14mg; Fibre 0.3g; Sodium 36mg.

VIENNESE WHIRLS

KEEN COOKS CAN HAVE THE CHANCE TO SHOW OFF THEIR SKILLS WITH THESE COOKIES. THE MIXTURE IS PIPED IN ROSETTE SHAPES ON TO A BAKING SHEET, THEN EACH PIECE IS SANDWICHED TOGETHER WITH SWEET, COFFEE-FLAVOURED BUTTERCREAM ICING. SERVE WITH MORNING COFFEE.

2 Spoon the mixture into a piping bag fitted with a 1cm/½in fluted nozzle.

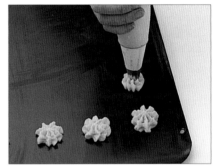

3 Pipe rosettes on greased baking sheets. Bake for 12–15 minutes until golden. Transfer to a wire rack to cool.

4 Put the coffee in a bowl. Heat the cream to near-boiling and pour it over. Infuse (steep) for 4 minutes, then strain.

MAKES 20

INGREDIENTS
   175g/6oz/12 tbsp butter
   50g/2oz/½ cup icing (confectioners')
      sugar
   2.5ml/½ tsp vanilla extract
   115g/4oz/1 cup plain (all-purpose)
      flour
   50g/2oz/½ cup cornflour (cornstarch)
   icing (confectioners') sugar and
      cocoa powder, to dust
For the filling
   15ml/1 tbsp ground coffee
   60ml/4 tbsp single (light) cream
   75g/3oz/6 tbsp butter, softened
   115g/4oz/1 cup icing (confectioners')
      sugar, sifted

1 Preheat the oven to 180°C/350°F/ Gas 4. Cream together the butter, icing sugar and vanilla extract until light. Sift in the flour and cornflour and mix together until smooth.

5 Beat together the butter, icing sugar and coffee cream. Use to sandwich the whirls in pairs. Dust with icing sugar and cocoa powder.

Energy 210Kcal/877kJ; Protein 2.2g; Carbohydrate 21.3g, of which sugars 11.2g; Fat 13.5g, of which saturates 7.6g; Cholesterol 22mg; Calcium 28mg; Fibre 0.8g; Sodium 64mg.

SUGAR COOKIES

THESE UNUSUAL LARGE COOKIES ARE MADE WITH A SWEETENED YEAST DOUGH SPICED WITH CINNAMON. THEY ARE EXTRA DELICIOUS SERVED WARM FROM THE OVEN, WITH THEIR CRUNCHY SUGAR COATING MELTING INTO THE FRAGRANT COOKIE DOUGH.

MAKES 5

INGREDIENTS
  250g/9oz/5 cups plain (all-purpose)
    flour, plus extra for dusting
  100g/3¾ oz/generous ½ cup sugar
  6ml/1¼ tsp easy-blend (rapid-rise)
    dried yeast
  pinch of salt
  5ml/1 tsp ground cinnamon
  30ml/2 tbsp full cream (whole) milk
  2 eggs, beaten
  100g/3¾oz/scant ½ cup unsalted
    butter, cubed and softened
  demerara (raw) sugar, for coating

1 Sift the flour into a large mixing bowl. Stir in the sugar, dried yeast, salt and cinnamon.

2 Whisk the milk and eggs together in a jug (pitcher). Make a well in the centre of the flour mixture and pour in the milk and eggs. Stir, incorporating the surrounding dry ingredients until the mixture holds together.

3 Add the softened butter, a few pieces at a time, and mix with your fingertips until all of it has been incorporated.

4 Shape the dough into a round and knead on a lightly floured surface for 10 minutes, until smooth.

5 Place the dough in a lightly oiled bowl, cover with clear film (plastic wrap) and leave to rest in the refrigerator for 1 hour.

6 Divide the dough into five pieces and, with your hands, roll each piece into a long roll. With a rolling pin, flatten each roll to a rectangle.

7 Sprinkle the demerara sugar on a plate. Press each piece of dough in turn in the sugar until coated all over. Place on a baking sheet lined with baking parchment and leave to rest for 20–30 minutes.

8 Preheat the oven to 190ºC/375ºF/ Gas 5. Bake the cookies for 20 minutes or until golden. Transfer to a wire rack. The cookies will harden as they cool. Break into pieces to serve.

GRANDMOTHER'S TIP
The cookies will keep for up to 1 week in an airtight container.

Energy 430kcal/1807kJ; Protein 7.6g; Carbohydrate 60.2g, of which sugars 22.1g; Fat 19.4g, of which saturates 11.2g; Cholesterol 119mg; Calcium 103mg; Fibre 1.6g; Sodium 154mg.

OAT BISCUITS

These crisp and crunchy biscuits are wonderfully quick and easy to make, as well as being utterly delicious. They are homely and comforting at any time of day, and are filling enough to keep hunger pangs at bay.

MAKES ABOUT 18

INGREDIENTS
    115g/4oz/½ cup butter
    115g/4oz/½ cup soft light brown
      sugar
    115g/4oz/½ cup golden (light corn)
      syrup
    150g/5oz/1¼ cups self-raising
      (self-rising) flour
    150g/5oz rolled oats

1 Preheat the oven to 180°C/350°F/Gas 4. Lightly grease or line two or three baking sheets with baking parchment.

2 Gently heat the butter, sugar and golden syrup in a heavy pan until the butter has melted and the sugar has dissolved, taking care not to let it burn.

3 Remove the syrup mixture from the heat and leave to cool, while you sift the flour. Stir in the flour to the butter, sugar and syrup mixture. Add the oats to the pan and mix together to make a soft dough.

4 Using your fingers, roll the dough into small balls and arrange them on the prepared baking sheets, leaving plenty of room for them to spread out.

5 Flatten each ball with a spatula. Bake for 12–15 minutes until golden brown, longer if more than one tray is in the oven.

6 Leave the biscuits to cool on the baking sheet briefly, then transfer to a wire rack to crisp up. Eat them warm, or cool completely before you store them.

VARIATION
Add 25g/1oz/¼ cup finely chopped toasted almonds, peanuts or walnuts, or a small handful of raisins, to the mixture in step 3.

Energy 151kcal/637kJ; Protein 1.8g; Carbohydrate 23.9g, of which sugars 11.9g; Fat 6g, of which saturates 3.3g; Cholesterol 14mg; Calcium 22mg; Fibre 0.8g; Sodium 59mg.

TOFFEE APPLE AND OAT CRUNCHIES

These soft cookies have an unsophisticated appeal, with their homely rough shape. The addictive mixture of chewy oats, soft apples and crunchy toffee pieces means they are top of the class for flavour. They could easily become children's lunch-box favourite.

MAKES ABOUT 16

INGREDIENTS
   150g/5oz/10 tbsp unsalted butter
   175g/6oz/scant 1 cup light
      muscovado (brown) sugar
   90g/3½oz/½ cup sugar
   1 large (US extra large) egg,
      beaten
   75g/3oz/⅔ cup plain (all-purpose)
      flour
   2.5ml/½ tsp bicarbonate of soda
      (baking soda)
   pinch of salt
   250g/9oz/2½ cups rolled oats
   50g/2oz/scant ½ cup sultanas
      (golden raisins)
   50g/2oz dried apple rings, coarsely
      chopped
   50g/2oz chewy toffees, coarsely
      chopped

1 Preheat the oven to 180°C/350°F/ Gas 4. Line two or three baking sheets with baking parchment.

2 In a large bowl, beat together the butter and both sugars until creamy. Add the beaten egg and stir well until thoroughly combined.

3 Sift together the flour, bicarbonate of soda and salt. Add to the butter, sugar and egg mixture and mix in well.

4 Finally add the oats, sultanas, chopped apple rings and toffee pieces and stir gently until just combined.

5 Using a small ice-cream scoop or large tablespoon, place heaps of the mixture well apart on the prepared baking sheets. Bake for about 10–12 minutes, or until lightly set in the centre and just beginning to brown at the edges.

6 Remove from the oven and leave to cool on the baking sheets for a few minutes. Using a metal spatula, transfer the cookies to a wire rack to cool completely.

Energy 249Kcal/1047kJ; Protein 3.1g; Carbohydrate 38.8g, of which sugars 23.2g; Fat 10.1g, of which saturates 5.3g; Cholesterol 32mg; Calcium 34mg; Fibre 1.3g; Sodium 79mg.

HONEY CRUNCH CREAMS

GREEK HONEY WORKS WELL IN THIS RECIPE, AS IT HAS A STRONG FLAVOUR OF LIQUORICE AND ANISEED. IF YOU PREFER A MORE SUBTLE TASTE, USE HEATHER OR LAVENDER HONEY. WHICHEVER YOU PREFER, MAKING THESE COOKIES WILL BRING AN AROMA OF THE COUNTRYSIDE TO THE KITCHEN.

MAKES 20

INGREDIENTS
    250g/9oz/2¼ cups self-raising
      (self-rising) flour
    10ml/2 tsp bicarbonate of soda
      (baking soda)
    50g/2oz/¼ cup caster (superfine)
      sugar
    115g/4oz/½ cup unsalted butter,
      diced
    rind of 1 large orange,
      finely grated
    115g/4oz/½ cup honey
    25g/1oz/¼ cup pine nuts or
      chopped walnuts
For the filling
    50g/2oz/¼ cup unsalted butter, at
      room temperature, diced
    115g/4oz/1 cup icing (confectioners')
      sugar, sifted
    15ml/1 tbsp honey

GRANDMOTHER'S TIP
It is best to use a dark, heavy honey for this recipe, with as much flavour as possible, so that the cookies really taste like honey.

1 Preheat the oven to 200°C/400°F/ Gas 6. Line three or four baking sheets with baking parchment. Sift the flour, bicarbonate of soda and caster sugar into a bowl. Add the butter and rub in until the mixture resembles breadcrumbs. Stir in the orange rind.

2 Put the honey in a small pan and heat until just runny but not hot. Pour it over the flour and sugar mixture and mix to a firm dough.

3 Divide the dough in half and shape one half into 20 small balls about the size of a hazelnut in its shell. Place the balls on the baking sheets, spaced well apart, and gently flatten.

4 Bake for 6–8 minutes, until golden brown. Leave to cool and firm up on the baking sheets.

5 Use a metal spatula to transfer the cookies to a wire rack to allow them to cool completely.

6 Shape the remaining dough into 20 balls and dip one side of each one into the pine nuts or walnuts. Place the cookies, nut sides up, on the baking sheets, gently flatten and bake for 6–8 minutes, until golden brown.

7 Leave to cool and firm up slightly on the baking sheets before carefully transferring the cookies to a wire rack, still nut sides up, to cool completely.

8 To make the filling, put the butter, sugar and honey in a small bowl and beat together until light and fluffy.

9 When the cookies are completely cool, use the filling to sandwich the cookies together in pairs using a plain one for the bottom and a nut-coated one for the top.

VARIATION
You could use chopped peanuts instead of pine nuts or walnuts, and sandwich the cookies together with peanut butter mixed with honey.

Energy 164Kcal/688kJ; Protein 1.5g; Carbohydrate 23.4g, of which sugars 13.9g; Fat 7.8g, of which saturates 4.4g; Cholesterol 18mg; Calcium 24mg; Fibre 0.4g; Sodium 52mg.

SHREWSBURY CAKES

DESPITE BEING KNOWN AS CAKES, THESE ARE ACTUALLY CRISP, LEMONY SHORTBREAD BISCUITS WITH PRETTY FLUTED EDGES, WHICH HAVE BEEN MADE AND SOLD IN THE TOWN OF SHREWSBURY IN ENGLAND SINCE THE 17TH CENTURY. THEY ARE SIMPLE TO MAKE AND INCREDIBLY ADDICTIVE.

3 Add the egg yolks to the butter and sugar mixture, one at a time, beating thoroughly after each addition.

4 Sift the flour over the top and add the lemon rind. Stir in and then gather up the mixture to make a stiff dough. Knead the dough lightly on a floured surface then roll it out to about 5mm/¼in thick.

5 Using a 7.5cm/3in fluted biscuit (cookie) cutter, cut out circles and arrange on the baking sheets. Gather up the offcuts and roll out again to make more biscuits.

6 Put into the hot oven and cook for about 15 minutes, until firm to the touch and lightly browned. Transfer to a wire rack and leave to crisp up and cool completely.

VARIATION
Omit the lemon rind and sift 5ml/1 tsp mixed (apple pie) spice with the flour in step 3.

MAKES ABOUT 20

INGREDIENTS
   115g/4oz/½ cup soft butter
   140g/5oz/¾ cup caster (superfine) sugar
   2 egg yolks
   225g/8oz/2 cups plain (all-purpose) flour, plus extra for dusting
   finely grated rind of 1 lemon

1 Preheat the oven to 180°C/350°F/Gas 4. Line two baking sheets with baking parchment.

2 In a mixing bowl, beat the softened butter with the sugar until pale, light and fluffy.

Energy 115kcal/482kJ; Protein 1.4g; Carbohydrate 16.1g, of which sugars 7.5g; Fat 5.4g, of which saturates 3.2g; Cholesterol 32mg; Calcium 23mg; Fibre 0.4g; Sodium 37mg.

CITRUS DROPS

THESE SOFT, CAKE-LIKE TREATS ARE DELICIOUSLY TANGY, WITH A CRUMBLY CITRUS-FLAVOURED BASE, FILLED WITH HALF A SPOONFUL OF LEMON OR ORANGE CURD BEFORE BAKING. THE CRUNCHY ALMOND TOPPING MAKES THE PERFECT FINISHING TOUCH. SERVE WITH A CUP OF COFFEE FOR ELEVENSES.

MAKES ABOUT 20

INGREDIENTS

175g/6oz/¾ cup unsalted butter, at room temperature, diced
150g/5oz/¾ cup caster (superfine) sugar
finely grated rind of 1 large lemon
finely grated rind of 1 orange
2 egg yolks
50g/2oz/½ cup ground almonds
225g/8oz/2 cups self-raising (self-rising) flour
90ml/6 tbsp lemon or orange curd
milk, for brushing
flaked (sliced) almonds, for sprinkling

1 Preheat the oven to 160°C/325°F/ Gas 3. Line two baking sheets with baking parchment. Beat the butter and sugar together until light and fluffy, then stir in the citrus rinds.

2 Stir the egg yolks into the mixture, then add the ground almonds and flour and mix well.

3 Divide the mixture into 20 and shape into balls. Place on the baking sheets. Make a hole in each cookie with the handle of a wooden spoon.

4 Put 2.5ml/½ tsp lemon or orange curd into each hole and pinch the opening to semi-enclose the curd.

5 Brush the tops with milk and sprinkle with flaked almonds. Bake for about 20 minutes until pale golden brown. Cool slightly on the baking sheets, then transfer to a wire rack.

Energy 157Kcal/658kJ; Protein 2.1g; Carbohydrate 16.8g, of which sugars 8.2g; Fat 9.6g, of which saturates 4.9g; Cholesterol 39g; Calcium 31mg; Fibre 0.6g; Sodium 55mg.

JAM TART BISCUITS

THESE SIMPLE BUTTERY BISCUITS FILLED WITH A SPOONFUL OF JAM ARE GIVEN AN EXTRA DIMENSION BY THE ADDITION OF THE SOUR CREAM TO THE MIXTURE. CHILDREN WILL LOVE TO HELP WITH THE CUTTING OUT OF THE DOUGH. MAKE PLENTY, AS THEY WILL BE POPULAR WITH ALL THE FAMILY.

MAKES 26–30

INGREDIENTS

100g/3¾oz/generous ½ cup caster (superfine) sugar
100g/3¾oz/scant ½ cup unsalted butter
1 egg
100ml/3½fl oz/scant ½ cup sour cream
350g/12oz/3 cups plain (all-purpose) flour, plus extra for dusting
5ml/1 tsp baking powder
90ml/6 tbsp raspberry jam

1 Preheat the oven to 180°C/350°F/ Gas 4. Put the sugar and butter in a large bowl and beat together until light and fluffy. Beat in the egg, then mix in the sour cream.

2 Sift the flour and baking powder together, then incorporate into the sugar, butter and egg mixture, which will have a fairly wet consistency.

3 On a lightly floured surface, roll out the dough to 5mm/¼in thickness then, using a floured 5cm/2in round cutter, cut out rounds and place on a baking tray. Leave to rest for 15 minutes.

4 Press down the centre of each round with your thumb or the back of a teaspoon, then spoon a little raspberry jam into the indentation.

5 Bake the biscuits (cookies) in the oven for 12–15 minutes, until golden. Transfer to a wire rack and leave to cool before serving.

Energy 711kcal/2992kJ; Protein 10.9g; Carbohydrate 110.7g, of which sugars 44.1g; Fat 28.1g, of which saturates 16.7g; Cholesterol 116mg; Calcium 173mg; Fibre 2.7g; Sodium 190mg.

APPLE CRUMBLE AND CUSTARD SLICE

THESE TASTY SLICES CLEVERLY COMBINE ALL THE INGREDIENTS OF A VERY POPULAR DESSERT INTO A COOKIE. THEY ARE VERY QUICK TO MAKE IF YOU USE READY-MADE SWEET PASTRY, BUT OF COURSE YOU CAN MAKE YOUR OWN PASTRY FROM SCRATCH BY ADDING A LITTLE SUGAR TO ANY SHORTCRUST RECIPE.

MAKES 16

INGREDIENTS
  350g/12oz ready-made sweet pastry
  1 large cooking apple, about
    250g/9oz
  30ml/2 tbsp caster (superfine) sugar
  60ml/4 tbsp ready-made thick
    custard
For the crumble topping
  115g/4oz/1 cup plain (all-purpose)
    flour
  2.5ml/½ tsp ground cinnamon
  60ml/4 tbsp sugar
  90g/3½oz/7 tbsp unsalted butter,
    melted

1 Preheat the oven to 190°C/375°F/Gas 5. Roll out the pastry and use to line the base of a 28 x 18cm/11 x 7in shallow cake tin (pan).

2 Prick the pastry with a fork, line with foil and baking beans and bake blind for about 10–15 minutes. Remove the foil and beans and return the pastry to the oven for a further 5 minutes until cooked and golden brown.

3 Meanwhile, peel, core and chop the apple evenly. Place in a pan with the caster sugar.

4 Heat gently until the sugar dissolves, then cover with a lid and cook gently for 5–7 minutes until a thick purée is formed. Beat with a wooden spoon and set aside to cool.

5 Mix the cold apple with the custard. Spread over the pastry.

6 To make the crumble topping, put the flour, cinnamon and sugar into a bowl and pour over the melted butter. Stir thoroughly until the mixture forms small clumps. Sprinkle the crumble over the filling.

7 Return to the oven and bake for about 10–15 minutes until the crumble topping is cooked and a golden brown. Leave to cool in the tin, then slice into bars to serve.

Energy 196Kcal/822kJ; Protein 2.1g; Carbohydrate 23.7g, of which sugars 8.1g; Fat 11g, of which saturates 4.9g; Cholesterol 15mg; Calcium 37mg; Fibre 0.9g; Sodium 124mg.

BRANDY SNAPS WITH CREAM

RECORDS SHOW THAT BRANDY SNAPS WERE SOLD AT FAIRS IN ENGLAND IN THE 1800S. THEY WERE CONSIDERED A SPECIAL TREAT FOR HIGH DAYS AND HOLIDAYS. EVERY KITCHEN HAD A LITTLE POT OF GROUND GINGER READY FOR ADDING TO CAKES, BISCUITS AND THESE LACY WAFER ROLLS.

3 Remove the pan from the heat. Sift the flour and ginger, and stir into the mixture with the brandy.

4 Put small spoonfuls of the mixture on the lined baking sheets, spacing them about 10cm/4in apart to allow for spreading. Put into the hot oven and cook for 7–8 minutes or until bubbling and golden. Meanwhile, grease the handles of several wooden spoons.

5 Allow the wafers to cool on the tin for about 1 minute then loosen with a metal spatula and quickly roll around the spoon handles. Leave to set for 1 minute, before sliding them off and cooling completely on a wire rack.

6 Just before serving, whip the cream until soft peaks form, spoon into a piping bag and pipe a little into both ends of each brandy snap.

GRANDMOTHER'S TIP
Unfilled brandy snaps will keep for a week in an airtight container.

MAKES ABOUT 12

INGREDIENTS
   50g/2oz/4 tbsp butter
   50g/2oz/¼ cup caster (superfine)
    sugar
   30ml/2 tbsp golden (light corn) syrup
   50g/2oz/½ cup plain (all-purpose)
    flour
   2.5ml/½ tsp ground ginger
   5ml/1 tsp brandy
   150ml/¼ pint/⅔ cup double (heavy)
    or whipping cream

1 Preheat the oven to 180°C/350°F/ Gas 4. Line two or three baking (cookie) sheets with baking parchment.

2 Gently heat the butter, sugar and golden syrup (in a pan on the stove or in the microwave on low power) until the butter has melted and the sugar has dissolved.

STRAWBERRY CREAM SHORTBREADS

THESE PRETTY TREATS ARE ALWAYS POPULAR, ESPECIALLY SERVED WITH AFTERNOON TEA OR AS A QUICK AND EASY DESSERT. SERVE THEM AS SOON AS THEY ARE READY BECAUSE THE SHORTBREAD COOKIES WILL LOSE THEIR LOVELY CRISP TEXTURE IF LEFT TO STAND.

SERVES 3

INGREDIENTS
150g/5oz/1¼ cups strawberries
450ml/¾ pint/scant 2 cups double
   (heavy) cream
6 round shortbread cookies

1 Reserve a few perfect and unblemished strawberries for decoration. Hull the remaining strawberries and cut them in half, discarding any bad parts.

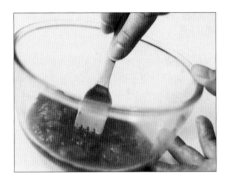

2 Put the halved strawberries in a bowl and gently crush them using the back of a fork. Only crush the berries lightly; they should not be reduced to a purée. A few larger chunks should still be left whole to add to the texture.

3 Put the cream in a large, clean bowl and whip until softly peaking. Add the crushed strawberries and gently fold in to combine. (Do not overmix.)

4 Halve the reserved strawberries – you can choose whether to leave the stalks intact or to remove them.

5 Spoon the strawberry and cream mixture on top of the shortbread cookies. Decorate each one with half a strawberry and serve immediately.

VARIATIONS
• You can use any other berry you like for this dessert – try raspberries or blueberries.
• Two ripe, peeled peaches will also give great results.
• Instead of shortbread, you can use freshly baked scones.

Energy 976kcal/4035kJ; Protein 5.7g; Carbohydrate 34.6g, of which sugars 16.8g; Fat 90.8g, of which saturates 50.1g; Cholesterol 206mg; Calcium 122mg; Fibre 1.3g; Sodium 204mg.

HONEY AND ALMOND BISCUITS

THESE DELECTABLE SPICED HONEY COOKIES WERE ONCE TRADITIONALLY MADE AT CHRISTMAS AS A SPECIAL SPICY TREAT. THEY ARE DELICIOUS SERVED WITH COFFEE, BUT ALSO MAKE A VERY GOOD ACCOMPANIMENT TO ICE CREAM, SORBETS, OR POACHED FRUIT DESSERTS.

MAKES 20

INGREDIENTS
    225g/8oz/1 cup clear honey
    4 eggs, plus 2 egg whites
    350g/12oz/3 cups plain
       (all-purpose) flour, plus extra for
       dusting
    5ml/1 tsp bicarbonate of soda
       (baking soda)
    2.5ml/½ tsp freshly grated nutmeg
    2.5ml/½ tsp ground ginger
    2.5ml/½ tsp ground cinnamon
    2.5ml/½ tsp ground cloves
    20 blanched almond halves

1 Beat together the honey and whole eggs until light and fluffy. Sift over the flour, bicarbonate of soda and spices, and beat to combine.

2 Gather the cookie dough into a ball, wrap in clear film (plastic wrap) and chill in the refrigerator for 1 hour or overnight.

3 Preheat the oven to 200°C/400°F/ Gas 6. Roll out the dough on a lightly floured surface to a thickness of 5mm/ ¼in. Using a 4cm/1½in cookie cutter, stamp out 20 rounds.

4 Transfer the rounds to two lightly greased baking trays. Beat the egg whites until soft peaks form. Brush the tops of the rounds with the egg white, then press an almond half into the centre of each one.

5 Place in the oven and bake for 15–20 minutes, or until they are a pale golden brown.

6 Remove from the oven and allow to cool slightly before transferring to a wire cooling rack. Leave to cool completely, then serve.

GRANDMOTHER'S TIPS
• In the days before sugar was widely available, honey was the only sweetener cooks had at their disposal. These little biscuits (cookies), sweetened only with honey, are a throw back to those far off days.
• Because there is no fat in the recipe, these biscuits will keep for up to 2 weeks in an airtight container.

Energy 112kcal/473kJ; Protein 3.4g; Carbohydrate 22.6g, of which sugars 8.9g; Fat 1.5g, of which saturates 0.4g; Cholesterol 38mg; Calcium 33mg; Fibre 0.5g; Sodium 22mg.

FRUIT TURNOVERS

BEFORE OVENS WERE INTRODUCED, TURNOVERS AND EVEN TARTS WERE COOKED ON THE GRIDDLE, AND IT MUST HAVE BEEN A SKILLED JOB TO GET THE TEMPERATURE JUST RIGHT AND TO FLIP THEM OVER WITHOUT LOSING THE FILLING. THIS RECIPE USES PLUMS, BUT YOU COULD USE APPLES OR JAM.

MAKES 8

INGREDIENTS
   450g/1lb plums, stones (pits)
     removed and chopped
   25–40g/1–1½oz/2–3 tbsp sugar
   350g/12oz/3 cups plain (all-purpose)
     flour, plus extra for dusting
   85g/3oz/6 tbsp lard or white cooking
     fat, cut into pieces
   85g/3oz/6 tbsp butter, cut into
     pieces
   milk and sugar for brushing and
     sprinkling
   pinch of salt

VARIATION
These turnovers work well with puff
pastry, too.

1 Bring the fruit and the sugar to the
boil with 15ml/1 tbsp water, then cover
and simmer for 5–10 minutes, stirring
frequently, until the fruit is soft. You
can reduce the liquid by bubbling
uncovered and stirring until thick.
Leave to cool.

2 Sift the flour and salt into a bowl,
add the lard or cooking fat and butter,
and rub them into the flour until the
mixture resembles fine crumbs
(alternatively, process in a food
processor).

3 Gradually stir in cold water until the
mixture forms clumps, then gather
together to make a smooth dough. Wrap
the pastry and chill for 20–30 minutes
to allow it to relax.

4 Preheat the oven to 190°C/375°F/
Gas 5. Then line a baking sheet with
baking parchment.

5 On a lightly floured surface, roll out
the dough to 3–5mm/⅛–¼in thick. Using
a small upturned bowl or plate as a
guide, cut out eight 15cm/6in circles,
re-rolling and cutting the pastry offcuts
as necessary.

6 Place a spoonful of cooled fruit on to
each pastry circle and brush the edges
with water. Fold the pastry over the
fruit, pinching the edges to seal them
well. Arrange the pastries on the
baking sheet, brush with milk, sprinkle
some sugar over and make a small
slit in each.

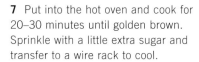

7 Put into the hot oven and cook for
20–30 minutes until golden brown.
Sprinkle with a little extra sugar and
transfer to a wire rack to cool.

Energy 340kcal/1420kJ; Protein 4.2g; Carbohydrate 38.5g, of which sugars 5.1g; Fat 19.8g, of which saturates 9.9g; Cholesterol 33mg; Calcium 66mg; Fibre 1.5g; Sodium 66mg.

SUFFOLK BUNS

CARAWAY SEEDS WERE ONCE A POPULAR INGREDIENT OF BREADS, CAKES AND SWEET CONFECTIONS, AND WERE OFTEN CHEWED TO SWEETEN THE BREATH. ENGLISH FARMERS TRADITIONALLY GAVE SEED CAKES AND BUNS TO THEIR LABOURERS AT THE END OF WHEAT SOWING.

4 Lightly beat the eggs and stir them into the flour mixture, together with sufficient milk to enable you to gather the mixture into a ball of soft dough. Transfer to a lightly floured surface.

5 Roll out to about 2.5cm/1in thick. Using a 5cm/2in biscuit (cookie) cutter, cut into rounds, gathering up the offcuts and re-rolling to make more.

6 Arrange the rounds on the lined baking sheet, setting them quite close together so they support each other as they rise.

7 Put into the hot oven and cook for 15–20 minutes until risen and golden brown. Transfer to a wire rack and dust with caster sugar. Leave to cool.

GRANDMOTHER'S TIP
Replace the caraway seeds with 50g/2oz dried fruit, such as raisins or finely chopped apricots.

MAKES ABOUT 12

INGREDIENTS
350g/12 oz/3 cups plain (all-purpose) flour, plus extra for dusting
115g/4oz/⅔ cup ground rice or semolina
10ml/2 tsp baking powder
115g/4oz/½ cup butter
75g/3oz/½ cup caster (superfine) sugar, plus extra for dusting
30ml/2 tbsp caraway seeds
2 eggs
about 75ml/5 tbsp milk

1 Preheat the oven to 200°C/400°F/ Gas 6. Line a baking sheet with baking parchment.

2 Sift the flour into a large mixing bowl, then add the ground rice and baking powder and mix to combine.

3 Add the butter to the flour mixture and, with your fingertips, rub it into the flour until the mixture resembles fine breadcrumbs. Stir the sugar and caraway seeds into the flour mixture.

Energy 244kcal/1026kJ; Protein 5.1g; Carbohydrate 36.9g, of which sugars 7.3g; Fat 9.5g, of which saturates 5.4g; Cholesterol 53mg; Calcium 60mg; Fibre 1.1g; Sodium 75mg.

WELSH CAKES

THESE CAKES WERE COOKED AT LEAST ONCE A WEEK IN KITCHENS TO ENJOY WITH A CUP OF TEA OR TO OFFER A TRADITIONAL WELCOME TO VISITORS. ORIGINALLY COOKED DIRECTLY ON THE SOLID PLATES OF RANGES, THERE ARE MANY VARIANTS OF THIS RECIPE. SERVE WARM, WITH BUTTER.

MAKES ABOUT 16

INGREDIENTS
  250g/9oz/2 cups plain (all-purpose)
    flour, plus extra for dusting
  7.5ml/1¼ tsp baking powder
  125g/4½oz/½ cup butter, cut into
    small cubes
  100g/3½oz/½ cup caster (superfine)
    sugar, plus extra for dusting
  75g/3oz/½ cup currants
  1 egg
  45ml/3 tbsp milk

1 Heat a bakestone or a heavy frying pan over medium to low heat.

2 Sift the flour, baking powder and salt into a large mixing bowl.

3 Add the butter to the flour mixture and, with your fingertips, rub it into the flour until the it resembles fine breadcrumbs. Alternatively, you can process the ingredients in a food processor. Stir the sugar and the currants into the mixture.

4 Lightly beat the egg, and with a round-ended knife and a cutting action, stir the egg into the flour mixture with enough milk to gather the mixture into a ball of soft dough.

5 Transfer to a lightly floured surface and roll out to about 5mm/¼in thick. With a 6–7.5cm/2½–3in cutter, cut out rounds, gathering up the offcuts and re-rolling to make more.

6 Smear a little butter or oil over the hot bakestone or pan and cook the cakes, in small batches, for about 4–5 minutes on each side or until they are slightly risen, golden brown and cooked through.

7 Transfer to a wire rack, dust with caster sugar on both sides and leave to cool a little before serving with butter.

Energy 128kcal/540kJ; Protein 4.1g; Carbohydrate 22.8g, of which sugars 1.3g; Fat 2.9g, of which saturates 1.4g; Cholesterol 29mg; Calcium 66mg; Fibre 0.9g; Sodium 29mg.

CHEWY FLAPJACKS

FLAPJACKS ARE POPULAR WITH ADULTS AND CHILDREN ALIKE, AND THEY ARE SO QUICK AND EASY TO MAKE. ALL SORTS OF EXTRA INGREDIENTS CAN BE ADDED TO THE BASIC MIXTURE, DEPENDING ON INDIVIDUAL TASTES, FROM CHOPPED APRICOTS OR RAISINS TO CHOCOLATE CHIPS AND NUTS.

SERVES 4

INGREDIENTS
   175g/6oz/¾ cup unsalted butter
   50g/2oz/¼ cup caster (superfine)
      sugar
   150g/5oz/generous ⅓ cup golden
      (light corn) syrup
   250g/9oz/2¾ cups rolled oats

1 Preheat the oven to 180°C/350°F/Gas 4. Line the base and sides of a 20cm/8in square cake tin (pan) with baking parchment.

2 Mix the butter, sugar and syrup in a pan and heat gently until the butter has completely melted.

3 Add the oats to the pan and stir until combined. Turn the mixture into the tin and level the surface.

4 Bake the flapjacks for about 15–20 minutes, until just beginning to turn golden. Leave to cool slightly, then cut into fingers and remove from the tin. Store in an airtight container.

Energy 241Kcal/1008kJ; Protein 2.7g; Carbohydrate 29.5g, of which sugars 14.3g; Fat 13.2g, of which saturates 7.2g; Cholesterol 30mg; Calcium 18mg; Fibre 1.4g; Sodium 125mg.

CHOCOLATE BROWNIES

THIS IS A CLASSIC TRAY BAKE THAT NEEDS TO BE SERVED CUT INTO SMALL PIECES, AS IT IS SO RICH. THE END RESULT SHOULD BE MOIST, DARK IN COLOUR WITH A CRUSTY TOP, AND SOFT ENOUGH TO EAT WITH A FORK OR SPOON. THESE BROWNIES ARE IMPOSSIBLE TO RESIST AT ANY TIME OF DAY.

MAKES 16

INGREDIENTS

  150g/5oz plain (unsweetened) chocolate, broken into squares
  120ml/4fl oz/½ cup sunflower oil
  215g/7½oz/1¼ cups light brown sugar
  2 eggs
  5ml/1 tsp vanilla extract
  65g/2½oz/⅔ cup self-raising (all-purpose) flour
  60ml/4 tbsp cocoa powder
  75g/3oz/¾ cup chopped walnuts or pecan nuts
  60ml/4 tbsp milk chocolate chips

1 Preheat the oven to 180°C/350°F/ Gas 4. Lightly grease a shallow 19cm/7½in square cake tin (pan). Melt the plain chocolate in a heatproof bowl over hot water.

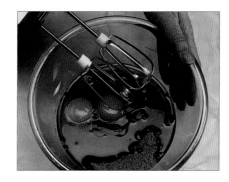

2 Beat the oil, sugar, eggs and vanilla extract together in a large bowl.

3 Stir in the melted chocolate, then beat well until evenly mixed.

GRANDMOTHER'S TIP
For a delicious dessert, warm these brownies slightly and serve with vanilla ice cream.

4 Sift the flour and cocoa powder into the bowl and fold in thoroughly.

5 Stir in the chopped nuts and chocolate chips, pour into the prepared tin and spread evenly to the edges.

6 Bake for 30–35 minutes, or until the top is firm and crusty. Cool in the tin before cutting into squares.

Energy 235Kcal/983kJ; Protein 3.4g; Carbohydrate 25.9g, of which sugars 22.2g; Fat 13.9g, of which saturates 3.8g; Cholesterol 25mg; Calcium 37mg; Fibre 1g; Sodium 49mg.

TOFFEE BARS

THREE LAYERS MAKE UP THIS WONDERFULLY IMPRESSIVE TRAY BAKE. THE SWEET DOUGH BASE IS TOPPED WITH A CARAMEL MIXTURE MADE WITH CONDENSED MILK, A STAPLE KITCHEN INGREDIENT IN DAYS GONE BY. MELTED CHOCOLATE IN THREE COLOURS ADDS THE FINAL LAYER.

MAKES ABOUT 24

INGREDIENTS
For the shortbread base
    250g/9oz/2¼ cups plain (all-purpose) flour
    75g/3oz/scant ½ cup caster (superfine) sugar
    175g/6oz/¾ cup unsalted butter, softened
For the filling
    90g/3½oz/7 tbsp unsalted butter, diced
    90g/3½oz/scant ½ cup light muscovado (brown) sugar
    2 x 397g/14oz cans sweetened condensed milk
For the topping
    90g/3½oz plain (semisweet) chocolate
    90g/3½oz milk chocolate
    50g/2oz white chocolate

1 Preheat the oven to 180°C/350°F/ Gas 4. Line and lightly grease a 33 x 23cm/13 x 9in Swiss roll tin (jelly roll pan).

2 Put the flour and caster sugar in a bowl and rub in the butter until the mixture resembles fine breadcrumbs. Work with your hands until the mixture forms a dough.

3 Put the dough into the prepared tin and press it out with your hands to cover the base. Then use the back of a tablespoon to smooth it evenly into the tin.

4 Prick all over with a fork and bake for about 20 minutes, or until firm to the touch and very light brown. Set aside and leave in the tin to cool.

5 To make the filling, put the butter, muscovado sugar and condensed milk into a pan and heat gently, stirring, until the sugar has dissolved.

6 Stirring constantly, bring to the boil. Reduce the heat and simmer the mixture very gently, stirring or whisking constantly, to prevent it sticking for about 5–10 minutes.

7 When the toffee filling has thickened and has turned a pale caramel colour, remove the pan from the heat. Take care that the mixture does not burn on the base of the pan, as this will spoil the flavour.

8 Pour the toffee filling mixture over the shortbread base, spread it evenly, then leave until cold.

9 To make the topping, melt each type of chocolate separately in a microwave or in a heatproof bowl set over a pan of hot water. Spoon lines of plain and milk chocolate over the set caramel filling.

10 Add small spoonfuls of white chocolate. Use a skewer to form a marbled effect on the topping. Allow to set, before cutting into squares.

Energy 305Kcal/1381kJ; Protein 4.6g; Carbohydrate 39.6g, of which sugars 31.6g; Fat 15.4g, of which saturates 9.6g; Cholesterol 37mg; Calcium 132mg; Fibre 0.4g; Sodium 120mg.

INDEX